"With all of the talk about what is to come there may be a tendency to slight, however unintentionally, the sacraments. Bill Huebsch's book, *Rethinking the Sacraments*, can be a corrective. With the changes brought about by Vatican II in mind and using a poetic style, he redefines and highlights what it is like to experience sacrament today."

Catholic Sun

"Bill Huebsch reminds us that authentic Catholic tradition is not the same as a dated routine. Seeing sacraments as 'holy moments in daily living' (better, perhaps, holy energies for daily living?) Huebsch reflects the best currents of contemporary theology. In short thought lines, he defuses some bad theology of the past and infuses sensible and challenging views that make sacraments really meaningful. Each sacrament is wisely seen in relation to the whole body of Christ, the social context."

Prairie Messenger

"Particular to the author's approach is his endeavor to declericalize and decentralize the sacraments and to incorporate 'these holy moments into everyday lives.' He succeeds in broadening views and providing a meditative forum for serious self-examination—a service to the church and all of us."

Spiritual Book News

"Huebsch is the readable popularizer of Catholic themes, utilizing typographical devices that make his thoughts look like poems—and often to read like poetry....Lots to ponder."

Edward O'Meara
Catholic Sentinel

BILL HUEBSCH

RETHINKING SACRAMENTS

Holy Moments
in Daily Living

XXIII
TWENTY-THIRD PUBLICATIONS
Mystic, Connecticut

Dedication

To my folks:
Herman Huebsch
and Margaret Fellerer Huebsch

Third printing 1991

Twenty-Third Publications
185 Willow Street
P.O. Box 180
Mystic CT 06355
(203) 536-2611
800-321-0411

ISBN 0-89622-393-0
Library of Congress Catalog Card Number 88-51812

Preface

The night was bitter cold, a late October night in a small town in rural Minnesota. I found my way to the local parish church and went inside, grateful to be out of the wind. They were ready for me: folding chairs, with the name of their patron saint stamped on the back panel, were standing in a semi-circle facing a podium and blackboard; the pastor was busy getting a prayer card ready; and a few folks were gathering in a corner talking quietly.

When I came into the room, they stopped talking.

The program started at 8:00 P.M. so the dairy farmers in the parish could finish their chores first. Out on the prairies above us was the fall corn crop, waiting to be hauled in for the winter. We were huddled together against a bitter fall night, the kind that assures you winter can't be far behind.

They hadn't yet turned the heat on in the church so the people were still wearing their coats. They looked to me like the huddled family in Van Gogh's painting, "The Potato Eaters." They were hard workers, struggling to survive in their rural economy while the world had become global in scale and electronic in speed. Their hard work and worry showed on their faces.

You could smell fresh egg coffee brewing back in the kitchen, and two women were back there putting homemade brownies on a tray.

Then we gathered and began. I started with a joke about how, if the diocese weren't charging such a large parish tax, they could turn their heat on before Christmas. No one laughed. I'd better get down to my point, I thought, before I lose them.

"Do you know what we're teaching your kids," I asked them, "about the sacraments?" Blank stares. I went into a brief panic, wondering whether I really wanted to tell them. I wondered whether they really even wanted to know, or cared to know.

"Do you remember what *you* were taught?" I was moving

on hopefully. "Come on," I pushed a little, "Baltimore Catechism question number 43 or so: 'What is a sacrament?'"

Some hands went up. "A sacrament is an outward sign, instituted by Christ, to give grace." A thin man in the back row. "You can leave," I told him, "Everyone else has to stay after class." A little laughter.

Aside from several good homilies over the years, a couple of articles in some of the Catholic press, and maybe something one of the kids brought home from CCD, that man hadn't heard a formal word about the sacraments since he was confirmed in the ninth grade. Or if he had, it hadn't been in any way that he could remember.

He'd seen a lot of change: the Mass was changed completely ("Everything but the collection," he said.) In fact, in that parish they no longer even called it Mass; they called it eucharist or liturgy or something.

Confession? What ever happened to confession, they wondered. "How come nothin's a sin anymore?" someone wanted to know.

Confirmation was still around, but the kids didn't memorize anything anymore.

Marriage? Still a sacrament but who cares? People just get divorces "fixed" now; someone's niece had gotten an annulment and the whole family was relieved.

Extreme unction? No one in the room knew whether it was still necessary to send for the priest at the time of death. "People die in hospitals," someone told me, "the nurses usually take care of that."

"I went to confession once," I said and paused on purpose. Everyone laughed. (I stole that pause from Gene LaVerdiere.) "No," I protested, "I meant that I went to confession once and on the way home I said to my mom from the back seat of the car, 'Well, Mom, I'm all clean now. I don't have any sins on my soul at all.' She turned around and said to me, 'That's presumption and that's a sin!'" Everyone liked that one; more laughter.

We began to talk about what we'd all learned and how we'd all grown up. The laughter and the memories began to emerge together. It wasn't a mocking laughter, though, but something more respectful and honest.

In the meantime, someone had found the switch for the furnace. People were taking their coats off and looking more comfortable.

There was a deep curiosity, and there were a lot of questions about what we are saying today about the sacraments and the church. These people had children and neighbors and, I got the feeling, some of themselves, too, in all kinds of irregular situations regarding various sacraments and the church in general.

"The family is where kids really learn about their faith," we keep saying: yet we haven't given the adults of the church more than a brief glimpse at what we're saying in twenty-five years.

But I find that it is possible to talk frankly about our needs, problems, joys, and successes in developing a sacramental life for the church. I find that people are eager to know about these things. But I also find that it needs to be presented more honestly. We have some problems; we have some challenges; we have diverse cultures around the world, diverse needs. Not everything we have done since Vatican II has worked well for us. Not everything done *at* Vatican II was done well either.

Why not honestly admit that we need to take another look at ways we pray and celebrate together? Why not probe a bit more, open the doors a bit, include everyone in the solution?

For example, confession. Very few people still go to individual confession often. Many don't go at all. But everything we used to teach about confession, now called reconciliation, seems to ignore our experience without admitting frankly that we have some problems here today and maybe we need to work at solving them together.

So I went on that night talking about these things as honestly as I could and telling them about what we're saying to their kids now. They were amazed. One of them said to me that it was about time someone brought them up to speed on this. I told them I'd come back again sometime. Within two weeks they'd booked another night.

Our Times

We live in a world facing tough times: nuclear insanity, economic hardship for whole nations, political insecurity around the world, wars springing up every week, and an ecological disorder that threatens our very air supply.

With all of this going on in our world, why would we want to talk about something so intramural as the sacraments of the churches?

The answer is simple and straightforward: this is our only hope. Global renewal can begin in only one place, Richard Malone has pointed out, and that place is the individual human heart.

The sacramental moments of life are holy moments, times that touch the heart, offer healing, unity, reconciliation, and courage. God can change history by transforming the human heart, the individual persons making all those individual changes, to renew the face of the earth.

So nothing is more timely than this, and nothing more urgent in the current life of the post-Vatican II church than an honest, frank refresher on this most central dimension of our life together: the sacraments.

The Format

I've chosen to present this in what I call "church basement language." It works there because it came from there in the first place. But I take pains to point out here again at the beginning that this presentation is purposely without every nuance of the greater theological arguments which form the basis of our thinking.

This is a "discussion draft" and is certainly not meant in any way to be the final word. Its purpose is, rather, to be kindling for the discussion. Respond to this, argue with me, disagree and say so! Look beyond this text and look into your hearts. Let this be another beginning, or maybe another end to something that should die.

The style of the prose here, like that of my former volume on wholeness and grace, is borrowed from ancient writers and, more recently, from Louis Evely. It's almost an oral writing; listen to the text as you read it. Let the words rise and fall and the white space on each page be a resting place for your thoughts.

Contents

Preface   *v*

What Is a Sacrament?   1

Remembering the Sacraments   7

Baptism   22

Confirmation   44

Eucharist   72

Reconciliation   96

Marriage   123

Holy Orders   146

Healing   175

Five More Sacraments   189

An Afterthought   193

What Is a Sacrament?

No one is quite sure
    how many sacraments there really are.
Some claim two or three,
    some seven,
    some more.
But, however they are numbered,
    it's important to realize
    that no sacrament
    started out being a sacrament.
That's right.
    Sacraments weren't invented by Christians
    from scratch.

Every sacrament has a long history
    in the human family.
Jews, Greeks, many ancient peoples
    remembered and commemorated
    these same moments
    of human life.
The rituals that we still celebrate
    and call sacraments today
    were part and parcel
    of ancient human customs.
Many religions used them:
    washing with water
    breaking and sharing bread
    pouring wine
    anointing with oil
    laying on of hands to bless and ordain
    calling down divine power
    pronouncing forgiveness

solemn commitments to lifelong vocations
blessing fire.

And these ancient peoples believed,
    as we do,
    that these rituals
    had tremendous divine power
        in their lives.
They believed that God,
    however they understood God,
    acted vigorously in these rituals.
And they believed that God
    was pleased by their actions
    when they gathered to do this.

It should be no surprise to us
    that this would be true.
These ancient peoples were only acting
    out of their human experience.
They recognized the holy moments of their lives
    and brought them into these rituals.
In a sense, then,
    these are natural moments,
    naturally religious points in life,
    naturally significant times
        that we bring to ritual
        in order to grasp more fully.
We bring them,
    as the ancient peoples did,
    because we cannot cope without doing so.

The early followers of Jesus Christ
    knew this in their bones.
They adopted these rites
    from their own lives
    and their own religious traditions
    and handed them on to us today.
Our own efforts to restore their power
    for us,

of which this work is a part,
must have this as a beginning point:
Sacramental moments are holy moments
and they are common to all humans.
They are not peculiarly Christian
and certainly not Catholic.
They tie us into the rich, profound
spirituality of the ages,
of our long human search for meaning.

In a sacramental moment,
we know from this long history,
two things happen:
we act
and God acts, too.
We come together,
our whole lives,
and we perform a drama,
a play.
We stage the significant moments,
acting out the parts,
and finding in the drama,
meaning.
And God steps into that human production
acting in our wills
forming our emotions
guiding our intellects
affecting our bodies.
In a word,
God graces us,
empowers us to be more completely whole.

We have a great human inheritance
in these sacramental moments,
a real opportunity
to tie into profound spirituality.

So the sacraments
are points of contact for us
with God.

We cannot see God
    but we can see fire;
    we can taste bread;
    we can hear words;
    we can smell incense;
    we can touch one another's bodies.
They are not ours alone,
    ours as Christians,
    but they belong,
        naturally,
        to all humans everywhere.
The heart of the sacraments is life itself.

God's love has been offered to us
    and received by us
    in Christ.
That is the Christ event.
This love will never be taken away:
    it's been given irrevocably.
The church is a sign of that giving
    of God's self to us.
It is a community
    founded on this giving of love,
        this power,
        this life,
        this grace.
Imperfect though the church is sometimes,
    tyrannical as its rulers sometimes are,
    less forgiving than Christ would be,
    less inclusive than the gospels,
    less unconditional than God,
still, mysteriously, the church goes on
    as that sign.
We go on because, as a group,
    we overcome the shortcomings
    of our individual members.
As a group,
    we are always filled with the Spirit
    even when individuals are not.

The purpose of the church, then,
    is not simply and soley
    to make it easier
    for people to find their individual salvation.
It does help do that,
    but people outside the church
    also find that salvation.
No serious person would any longer claim
    that only those who've been baptized
    will be "saved."
The church has no corner on the market
    of eternal life—
    sorry.

But Karl Rahner has helped us understand
    that there is one thing
    that is not possible without the church:
    that God's grace be present in the world
        in a physical
        tangible
        audible way.
On the bottom line, that's it:
    the church isn't rules and regulations,
        do's and don'ts,
        a cold and impersonal set of laws.
It isn't the clergy and religious alone;
    it isn't the people in the pews alone.
The church is the living event
    of God's presence.
It is people who've been touched by God
    and who have come to realize that;
    people graced and loved by God
    who now return in worship and awe.
To be a member of the church
    is to be one of these:
    one who becomes part of the acting out
        of the mystery of God.
It is to be one who sees beyond the ordinary
    into the love of God.

It is, as Rahner says, to believe that
     bread and wine
     oil and water
     sex and prayer
          can carry this love
          and make it real in our day.
It is to turn in service to one another
     as sisters and brothers,
     to wash each others' feet,
          to try to return love for love.

The sacraments are the moments
     of our being together in the church
     that give us the chance
     for this meaning.
They are the times when we mean what we do
     and become what we mean.
They are high points of celebration,
     moments of grace,
     opportunities for empowerment.
And because they form such an integral part
     of being church for us,
          we want to talk about them here.

Remembering
the Sacraments

There are some things about the sacraments
that everyone should know.

If there is one question
in the Baltimore catechism
that all of us remember,
it is the one which asked,
"What is a sacrament?"

The answer to this question
was pressed into our memories
for eternity.
Nothing was more important
to our teachers
than that we understand
and could recite
answers about the sacraments.

The problem, of course,
was that while we had the answers,
the questions didn't always
seem that important to us.
We were young
and we had other things
on our minds.
But nonetheless we learned the answers:
"A sacrament is an outward sign
instituted by Christ
to give grace."

Why was this so important?
Because, in a sense,
    the sacraments *are* the church.
They are,
    for most of us,
    the actual point of contact
    with others who are Christian.
They are the moment in which
    we encounter the church-assembled.
They are the times of gathering
    as a parish community.
They are when we see the others
    who are walking with us.
They are when we talk about churchy things,
    when we sing religious songs,
    when we pray out loud together,
    and when we come forward publicly
        to be seen as part of this church.

When I was a kid,
    in the "good old days,"
    we used to talk about "going to church"
        on Sunday.
What we meant, of course,
    was that we were going to Mass.
We so identified going to church
    with going to Mass
        that, in our way of thinking,
        they were one and the same.
So, after Vatican II,
    when the officials started
    tinkering and changing the Mass,
    it felt to us
        like they were changing the whole church.
To us the Mass *was* the whole church.

And that's how it was for most Catholics then.
But today we have some new perspectives
    on all of this.
Today when we talk about Mass,

we speak of "liturgy"
or "eucharist."
It isn't the Mass which is the church;
it is *us* who are the church.
The Mass is one part of that,
a very important part,
but not all of it.

So in those "good old days"
we were accustomed
to receiving the sacraments.
The language betrayed our real understanding.
We *received* them,
we were inactive observers of the rites
and, when the appropriate time came,
we would go up front
or into a box
and have something done to us
by the priest
who administered the sacraments.
We didn't really have to do anything
but be there
in the right place
at the right time.
It happened to us;
we didn't have much to do with it.

The sacraments we received in this way
were seven,
a magical number for Christians
as well as for many other
of the world religions.
The seven sacraments were known by everyone
to be complete.
Receiving them was what made one
a "practicing Catholic":
baptism
penance
holy communion

confirmation
matrimony
holy orders
extreme unction.

Knowing that these sacraments
    were there
    provided us with a distinct sense
    of comfort.
The church was home to us:
We knew our way around,
    we knew what to expect there,
    we were very seldom surprised
    by what anyone said or did in church.

But that has changed.
Today I doubt that anyone
    would wager on what might happen
    in some churches on a given Sunday morning.
Today there is a great deal of surprise
    and change,
    and we don't have the same sense
    of being "at home" there.

There is, therefore,
    a certain discomfort
    in the church today
    about the sacraments.
We used to understand them,
    or at least we thought we did.
We had, after all, memorized those answers
    in the Baltimore catechism.
But today there is a general feeling around
    that those answers have changed,
    and we aren't really sure what the
        changes are.

Confession

When our kids ask us about
    confession, for example,
    we try to tell them what we know,
    but we get caught in our words
        and we realize,
        even as we speak,
        that we ourselves
        have stopped using this sacrament.
It's hard to teach your kids
    to do something that you yourself
    have already stopped doing.
So we feel a little guilty,
    and we tell ourselves that we really
        should start going to confession again,
        but we never seem to get around to it.
We seem, in fact,
    to be getting along pretty well without it.
But still the doubts nag us;
    they won't go away.

Matrimony

The same is true of matrimony.
All of us know people who got married
    and then, for some reason,
    the marriage just didn't work out;
    and they got divorced.
We really don't blame them.
We say to ourselves that we know
    how things happen;
    we feel for them,
        and we don't want to judge them.
So these people get re-married,
    usually without an annulment;
    and we find ourselves
    being secretly kind of happy for them.

Of course,
>   we know, officially,
>   that they are living in sin!

But we are happy that they were able
>   to find love in their lives again,
>   that they aren't alone any longer,
>   that things are picking up,
>   that they have a second chance.

And we really hope that this time
>   it'll work out better.

But then what does the sacrament of matrimony
>   really mean?

What happens to all those people,
>   hundreds of thousands of them,
>   who aren't "legally" married
>   in the eyes of the church?

Isn't that a mortal sin?
>   And if they die in mortal sin,
>   don't they go to...?!

We don't know, so we just try not to think
>   about it very much.

Baptism

And then there's baptism.

We were taught
>   that unbaptized people who die
>   never go to heaven.

So we try to hurry and have our babies
>   baptized.

We don't want them spending eternity in Limbo,
>   wherever that is.

But still,
>   we wonder.

What happens to Jews who die?
>   Do they go to Limbo, too?

And what about Buddhists and Hindus?

Moslems?
Did Gandhi go to Limbo?
What happens to all the communists
    when they die?

Do we really still teach this?
I once knew a pastoral care worker
    in a large Catholic hospital
    who zealously carried a cotton swab
        in her smock.
Anytime someone neared death
    whose chart indicated anything
    but a Christian background,
    she would dampen the swab
        and baptize the patient
        with a few drops of water.
When she couldn't reach the forehead,
    she'd hit the elbow or foot,
    any part that she could reach.
She did this
    out of charity
    in order to help these people reach heaven.
But she was misdirected. Wasn't she?

Extreme Unction

The one sacrament
    we might have thought would be sacred
    would be extreme unction.
I mean,
    this is the "last chance" sacrament,
    and not one
    with which we should mess around.
Death, after all,
    is permanent and we shouldn't take
    any last minute chances.
But something is going on here, too.

When we were kids,
    in those "good old days" again,
    we all wore little medals around our necks.
These medals were really a sort of
    Catholic dog tag.
They carried a picture of a saint,
    but they also carried a message
    for whoever would find us at the
    moment of our death:
        "I am a Catholic.
        In case of an accident,
            please call a priest."
It was very important that Father be there
    at the moment of our death.

But today something funny is going on here,
    and we aren't sure what.
Every now and then
    there is an announcement in the bulletin
    that there will be a service
    that afternoon
        to celebrate the sacrament of healing.
"The sacrament of healing?" we ask.
    "Where did this come from?"
"This wasn't one of the original seven,
    was it?"
If you've ever gone to one of these
    afternoon celebrations of this sacrament,
    you could easily see that
    not everyone in the room,
        or maybe no one,
        was near death.
This is confusing: all these people
    coming to church on a Sunday afternoon,
    publicly asking for healing
        from emotional
        physical
        relational
    or spiritual pain.

Publicly asking for healing
   is embarrassing,
   so we generally keep our distance
   and prefer to just wait,
      taking our chances that the priest
      will be able to make it
      at the moment of our death.

Holy Communion

And what about holy communion?
   There was a time when we fasted
   from midnight, or at least three hours,
   each time we received.
Now they serve coffee and doughnuts
   before the Mass,
   and they tell us that we should visit
      with the people sitting around us.
And then there's the matter
   of receiving outside the state of grace.
I know that most people don't
   go to confession as often as they should,
   and I just bet that some people
   go to communion
      with or without confession!
The Mass used to be laden
   with incense
   chimes
   candle light
   and Latin.
It was a mysterious and very holy moment
   in the week ,
   and one that no one took lightly.
Every good Catholic went to Mass
   every Sunday.
Now people seem to go when they want to.
Has something changed here
   that they didn't tell us about?
   I wonder.

Holy Orders

In the old days,
    if there was one profession you could trust,
    it was the priesthood.
The parish was the center of life,
    and the priest was the center of the parish.
Getting ordained
    meant moving to a realm
    that was almost beyond the human.
But sometime in those turbulent 1960s
    something changed here.
Priests started leaving the priesthood,
    marrying nuns,
    or whoever.
They started carrying picket signs
    in anti-war protests,
    civil rights marches,
    and gay pride parades.
What was happening?
Is nothing sacred?
    we wonder.

Confirmation

It's almost possible to forget this last one,
    confirmation.
We don't know for sure what this does.
Baptism ushers us in, we know;
    and extreme unction ushers us out;
    matrimony and holy orders
        commit us for life;
    confession and communion take us
        through the weeks and months and years.
But what does confirmation really do?
Officially, it's part of being initiated
    into the church;
    but the way it's administered in most places,

it's more of a graduation
than an initiation!
Most young people see it as the
grateful end
of high school religious education.
We really need to do some work on this.

And on and on....
The sacraments just aren't what they used to be!

We need to talk about this, though,
and we shouldn't wait much longer.
We need to look at the sacraments,
whether it's seven or eight or nine;
it really doesn't matter.
We need to think again about what they mean,
and we need to find a language
that expresses our beliefs.

We began here by saying
that the sacraments are the way,
that they *are* the church.
They are our heritage,
our common legacy,
our only real way to touch the divine.
They are ours
but we feel that we've lost them
somehow.
How can we get them back?
How can we teach them to our kids?
How can we make them meaningful again
for ourselves?

We're going to spend some time here
looking at all of this again.
As adults,
we need to know these things,
we need to re-learn our catechism,
so that we can make the sacraments
a vital part of our lives again.

One thing we'll find,
    as we do this,
    is that less has changed
    than we think.
What we used to teach is not wrong today
    and what we're saying now
    is not new.
Before our current renewal in the church
    each sacrament had a focus,
        an emphasis,
        a primary stress.
This focus was established and maintained
    mostly by the priests and sisters
    who taught religion.
That focus has shifted today,
    but it is a focus shift
    not a new theology.
Actually
    what we're saying today
    about each of these sacraments
        is old.
Many of these new points of focus
    were once observed in an earlier age,
    and we are returning to them now.

The outward signs haven't changed at all:
    We still use water in baptism
    bread and wine at communion
    oil in confirmation
    and words in confession.
The role of Christ in instituting them
    hasn't changed,
    although our understanding
    of what that means
        has developed.
And how they give grace

continues to pour life into the church.
Only today
we use different words
to describe how that happens.

So what's changed?
Really,
when it comes down to it,
we are what's changed.
We've undergone a thorough
cultural housecleaning as a church
and as a society,
and we've learned two important lessons
from that.
First, Ted Ross, the Jesuit historian,
has helped us understand that
authentic Catholic tradition
is not the same as
a dated Catholic routine.
Our traditions are sacred:
They give meaning to our lives.
How would it be if we failed,
for example,
to use bread at eucharist?
How could we call that eucharist?
Bread is a tradition.
But the white cloth on the communion rail
under which we used to place our hands
when we received the bread—
that is routine.
It was a dated practice
and had lost all meaning for us.
It would be tough to receive
communion in your hand
if your hand was beneath an altar cloth.

Authentic tradition we keep;
dated routine we dump.

The second major lesson we've learned
   is that the revealed truth of God
   is not the same
      as the academic words
      we use to express it.
The words we use,
   human and limited as they are,
   can never adequately
      express the truths of God.
How could they? We aren't God.

So, while the words of one generation
   seem to express God's truth
   well enough for that generation,
   Ted Ross has pointed out that
      they will almost certainly
      be a stumbling block for the next.

Revealed truth does not change.
Our ways of expressing it must change
   or they will whither and die.

The prayers of the Mass,
   for example,
   uttered in Latin and
   understood by no one, save the priest,
   served the church beautifully
   for several generations.
But few would argue that today
   our role in the Mass
   could not properly be exercised
      without using our own language.
The words have changed,
   but the truths remain the same.

We will be examining all of this here:

what we are saying today
the words we are using
the revealed truths that we believe
the changes that have emerged
the dated routine that's been removed
and the authentic traditions that go on.

This will help us find a deeper
understanding
and meaning
in this sacramental heritage of ours.

Regaining a sacramental life
for ourselves and our parish is exciting
because it restores the flow of grace
that we have long lived without
as our sacramental life has diminished.
It's exciting because it's energizing.

So it's time to talk again
about the sacraments of Christ
because there are some things
about this
that everyone should know.

For Reflection and Discussion
Read the Preface and "What Is a Sacrament?"
1. Share memories of learning about sacraments.
   •What do you still remember?
   • What do you still believe?
2. Share your sacramental history:
   •when, where, from whom, with whom?
3. What questions do you have now about the sacraments.

Baptism

Almost no one
    can remember their baptism,
    which is not true
    for the other sacraments.
Most of them
    leave a memorable impression
    on us:
Who could forget their
    first time in the
    old confessional box?
Or who has lost the memory
    of their first communion?
We tend to really celebrate
    weddings and ordinations,
    making them unforgetable events in our lives.
Confirmation,
    even though not very well understood,
    is a big family event.
Even the "last rites"
    make a lasting impression,
    especially if you don't die
        after all.
But baptism is forgetable,
    for the most part.

That's because we're baptized as babies
    rather than as adults.
We have a sense of what it must have been like
    when we ourselves were baptized
    because we have a much better recollection
    of the baptisms of others
    than we do our own.

But the babies we're baptizing
    will soon forget,
    just as we have.

So what happens at baptism
    that's so important?
Is baptism something
    that we do to babies
    in order to keep them from Limbo?
Or is there more to it than that?

It's important for us to
    talk about this.
Baptism,
    after all,
    is the sacrament that, we are told,
    empowers us as "ministers."
We keep hearing that baptism
    is such a key,
    such a central,
    such an essential sacrament.
We're sure this is true,
    but since we can't remember,
    and we haven't been taught much,
    we feel a little in the dark.
And,
    when it comes right down to it,
    and we honestly admit
    how we feel and think about it,
        we have to admit
        that we do not experience baptism
        as anything but
        something we know
        happened "to us" once
            when we were babies.
In our heads we know it was important,
    but in our experience of life,
    it doesn't seem to matter that much.

The other sacraments are different:
    they're loaded with hoopla
    and schamltz;
    we usually do them up in a big way!
And they have an immediate impact in our lives:
    they're vital for us.
But baptism is old hat;
    it happened for most of us
    so long ago
    that it doesn't seem to matter much now.

The only real contact
    that most of us have with our baptism
    in our adult lives
    is the renewal of baptismal promises
    that we do each year
    on Holy Saturday night.
But it seems strange to us:
    "Do you reject Satan?"
We mutter our way through the responses,
    provided we found the right page
    in the missalette,
        and it ends up that we aren't touched
        that deeply or profoundly.
We're quite sure that we *do* reject Satan,
    but isn't there more to it than that?

There is some confusion about
    baptism today.
We don't intend to clear that up here,
    but it *is* possible for us
    to get a clearer focus,
    a better footing,
    and a deeper appreciation
        for whatever did happen to us
        on the day we were baptized.

The confusion,
    at least in part,

stems from the fact that there are
two aspects to baptism
    which, when mixed together,
    seem troublesome.
First,
    baptism is for adults:
It is the end of a journey
    to faith in Christ;
    it is the final "yes,"
    a faith-filled response,
    a decision to become a full member
        of the followers of Christ.
In the early church,
    this meant years of study,
    and working a serious program
        of turning one's life over to Christ.
It meant knowing the Scriptures,
    taking on a ministry in Christ's name,
    and making a solemn vow
        to remain faithful for life.
It was a decision that only an adult could make,
    and it was not undertaken lightly.

But second,
    baptism is for kids.
It is entering into a life,
    even as an infant,
    of being brought up in the church,
    a community of people
        committed to being for Christ.
This means that the family,
    parish,
    circle of friends,
    and even the strangers in church,
        become the seedbed for faith
        so that,
        from the earliest years of life,
        a child is "in Christ."
Being "in Christ" means

caring for one another
    without counting the cost;
listening to ourselves
    and accepting the truth we find there;
reflecting and praying often,
    alone and with others;
giving good news and food to the poor;
    proclaiming release to captives,
    recovery of sight to the blind,
    freedom to those bound in themselves,
    and proclaiming Jesus as Lord.
Now this is not something
    that a baby can do.
But it is something that a baby can learn
    as a way of life
    only by being raised among other folks
    who have it as their goal.

So there we have it:
    baptism is for adults,
    but baptism is for kids.

How do we resolve this?
Let's start with the kids
    and then move on to the adults,
    gaining perspective as we go.

Baptism is for kids.
Being born is no fun
    either for mother or for child.
For the mother
    there are months of waiting
    which end in painful moments
    of birthing.
Even when the birthing is by surgery,
    there is pain and trauma.
It's no picnic for the mother.

But our perspective here is going to be

from the point of view of the child
at birthing time.

The birthing begins really
    at conception
    when the code of life
    contained in the fiber of the cells
    is set to determine a person.
No one knows the exact time;
    it is a lonely moment for the child.
A human person is being made,
    and no one even knows it.
    A great shared power
        is at work:
        human and divine,
        but it works in secret.
The child is at once
    unknown
    and yet fully at home.

And there,
    nestled in the warmth and darkness,
    something begins to stir,
    cells multiply,
        not haphazardly,
        but exactly planned.
There, in the comfort of that place,
    the first days
        and weeks
        and months
    of life are spent
    in preparation for birthing
    and whatever will follow.
There has been no pain to bring this about,
    no suffering,
    no shedding of blood
        as there will be at birthing.
Rather,
    for most babies

there is safety and security
and waiting.

But then every good thing must come to an end,
as they say,
and birthing is inevitable.
Comfortable as it may be,
the time comes when discomfort
is the way to birth.

And so it begins:
The safety and security
of the womb
is replaced with
the risks and responsibilities
of the world.
A child is born into a world,
a place in history
beset with needs and difficulties.
That world,
no doubt,
is also filled with awe and wonder.
But unlike the silent consent of conception,
birthing is loud and confusing.
In a word,
birthing raises a ruckus!

Our topic here,
we must remember,
is not birthing but baptism.
This child is born unbaptized,
that is our point;
and what that means for us
is our next concern.
The child is born with original sin.

Remember original sin?
Jim Lopresti has said
that original sin has been "closed"
—for repairs!

There is a bit of misunderstanding
    about original sin
    that we should clear up
    in order to fully understand baptism.

When we were kids
    going to catechism class,
    many of us were taught
    that every human being
        at the time of birth
        was somehow guilty of sin.
We sort of believed that babies
    were born in sin.
That's an awful thought,
    that a baby is born in sin,
    but thankfully
    it's more a popular belief
    than an official teaching of the church.
This notion that babies are born in sin
    had a loose connection
    to the religious idea
    that sex is a sin:
sex and reproduction and all that stuff.

We've had a hard time to find much
    divine glory in this,
    but more and more we can see
    that God gave us sex and fruitfulness
        as the crowning moment
        of all creation.
"Be fruitful and multiply and fill the earth."
All of this was God's idea,
    and it must be good.

But that thought aside for the moment,
    we must insist,
    as our starting point,
    that babies are not born in sin.
They are not personally guilty
    of anyone else's sins either.

But,
    mysteriously,
    they do have an inner condition,
    common to all humans,
    which renders them subject to sin.
This inner condition
    is not itself a freely chosen
    rejection of God
    but rather this:
        we are, all of us,
        subject to darkness.
We do not know ourselves;
    we do not love perfectly;
    we do not choose truth without pain,
        good without difficulty,
        right without doubt.
There is something going on inside us
    which,
    as Paul said it,
    makes us choose the very things
    we do not want to choose.
It is not that we are born evil
    but that we are born
    with the possibility of choosing evil.

The inner human condition
    that gives rise to this possible choice
    of darkness and sin,
    that inner condition, is our original sin.
It isn't a sin
    in the sense that it is a freely chosen
    rejection of God,
    the kind of sins we commit as adults.
Really, it is more accurate to say that it
    resembles sin
    and gives rise to the possibility of sin.
It is, in a sense,
    an admission that, as human beings,
    we have lost our innocence.

The story of Adam and Eve
    helps us understand this.
In that story,
    the people were given many gifts,
    everything they needed for life.
In a sense,
    that time was a womb time,
    a time when everything is provided
    and we do not need to worry.
They had all that,
    but instead of using the gifts of the garden
        for good,
        for relating,
        for sharing with one another,
    they chose to be selfish.
Instead of being relational,
    they became unilateral.
That was their sin.

The story of Adam and Eve is true,
    literally true,
    but it is true about us,
        not about them.
The choice to be unilateral or relational,
        selfish or generous,
        sinful or graceful,
        in darkness or in light—
    that is the awful choice
    that we must make.

Now we know that no baby
    born only days earlier,
    can make such a choice.
We do not believe or teach
    that such a child is in sin.
But they are born with that inner condition
    which makes it necessary for them
    to face that awful choice
    between light and darkness.

Here, though,
      is the real key to baptism
      because that's not all babies are born with,
      and it's not even the most important thing.
Babies are also born with grace.

Grace is a power we receive
      from God,
      a power that enables us to know ourselves
      in ways that animals don't.
It's an orientation toward God
      that is present in each of us
      from the very beginning.
That grace is part of being human.
Their very birth itself is
      a moment of grace.
Like all humans,
      they do not have at birth
      all the grace they need;
      but they are born in grace,
            there's no doubt about it.

Baptism celebrates that:
      It celebrates the "other condition"
      that is present there,
      the condition of grace.

Baptism empowers that child
      to choose truth
            goodness
            beauty
            and right.
The ancient ritual of pouring water
      unites that child
      with the spiritual forces of the ages
      in a history-long struggle
      to overcome darkness
      with the light of the Great Spirit.
By itself,

the child
and the world do not stand a chance.
By itself,
    the child
    is isolated and alone.
Baptism,
    we might say,
    awakens within the child
    the grace implanted there by God
    to be united with Christ
        and, thereby,
        united with the body of Christ as well.
Baptism initiates that child into the church.

But there is more.
There is a deep inner power released
    at the pouring of the water,
    but there is also
    something happening to the others present.
Baptism doesn't affect only the newly baptized.
The others present at this moment
    find themselves mysteriously linked
    to a great spiritual force.
They are, in a sense,
    refreshed themselves
    in their own inner life.
They are not re-baptized,
    (we are claimed for Christ only once),
    but they are re-empowered
        and re-united to Christ.

So babies are born in the state of grace,
    but they are also born without grace.
They are born in the state of grace
    because of Christ's life.
That life,
    once and for all,
    empowers us to live ourselves,
        as he did,
        in the energy of God.

But they are born without grace
        because we are human after all:
        and, as Christ has shown,
        we must pass through death
            in order to be fully alive.
So this child,
        having all the possibility of full life,
        must also cope with a difficult world.

Babies, after all,
        are born into a sinful world.
And they are born
        with that awful power to choose
        between life and death.
So the other side of baptism
        is that it brings us
        first and foremost
        into a group of people who are also
            facing that same terrible choice.
If only we didn't have that freedom!

But we do and we're glad of it, really.
And in just the same way
        that we learn,
        through the story of the garden,
        about the pull from both sides,
        so we in our day also find both
            the light of Christ
            and the darkness of sin
                appealing.
Baptism,
        besides giving us an inner power
        also gives us one another.
So baptism,
        really,
        is for adults.

Baptizing babies is easy,
        but living a baptized life as an adult
        is not.

This part of what we have to say here
　　will make us uncomfortable,
　　I think,
because it pushes us to take seriously
　　what we do to our children.

I don't know how long it's going to take us
　　to figure out
　　that we need one another.
Children understand this pretty well,
　　and older people do, too.
But it's the big, independent bunch
　　in the middle years
　　that forget this.
It's those folks
　　who are financially independent
　　socially secure
　　domestically settled
　　and generally able to take care
　　　　of themselves.
It's those folks
　　who think they can also be
　　emotionally independent
　　and spiritually private.
It's them,
　　the other guys and gals,
　　those folks;
but really it's *we*,
　　isn't it?
We continually choose to go it alone,
　　to be unilateral,
　　to repeat the story of the garden.
What's our problem?
Can't we get it into our heads
　　that being human means
　　being together?
Every Sunday,
　　all over the country,
　　we have churches full of people

who,
    even though they're in church,
    are still trying to go it alone.
Even though we're all baptized,
    still we are alone.

The story from Genesis
    of the man and woman in the garden
    is a story of people like us
    whose relationship was ruptured
        by selfishness
        greed
        a love for power
        and a unilateral way of living.
Those ruptured relationships
    are at the core of our own sin.
They are also at the core
    of poverty
    war
    sickness
    meanness
    terrorism
    loneliness
        and pain.
But we don't have to live like that.
We do have another choice.

We have too long been taught,
    I think,
    that what happens at baptism
    is complete.
We have been taught
    that, once we're baptized,
    it's over,
        that we've got all we're gonna get
        from God.
But that's not true.
Perhaps more than any other,
    baptism is a sacrament
    that stays with us.

It's a sacrament that continually
forms us and molds us.

Being baptized into Christ
is being united with him
in that struggle to undo
what was first done in the garden.
It means that we become relational.

It means,
in short,
that we become part of one another,
learn to care for one another,
provide generously for one another,
share ourselves freely.
It means that our first priority
cannot be getting rich
or famous
or smart
or powerful
or pleasureful.
Our first priority
becomes that of Christ,
to join with others
in order to love them.

So, even though we're baptized as babies,
we still must give our adult selves
to Christ.
And we do that by giving our adult selves
to one another
in community.
But how long will it take us to realize this?
How long will it take us
to turn to one another,
not for profit
not for pleasure
not for power
but in love?

How long will it take us to realize
    that this deep longing
    for affection and love that we have,
    this longing for companionship and care,
    this longing is a longing for Christ.
It is the deer that longs for running streams;
    it is us.

There is a story in the gospel
    that brings all this to light
    in a very poignant
    and stirring way.
It is the story of a blind man
    and it's in the gospel of Mark.
In the story,
    this guy is sitting along a road
    and the text tells us
    that he is a blind beggar.
Now, as soon as you hear that,
    you probably say to yourself
    that this must be a story about
        someone else.
Surely it couldn't be a story about you!
After all,
    you aren't a blind beggar, are you?
Well, listen up!
    This is a story about us,
    about being blind the way we are
    and about begging the way we do.
You see,
    the thing about being blind is
    that you can't see what you can't see.
So we are sometimes blind
    and don't even know it
    and that's the kind of blindness
        that this story is about,
        the kind that you and I have.

The story says that this blind guy
    was sitting alongside the road.

He really wasn't going anywhere,
    he was stalled,
    stopped,
    and staid.
And his name was Bartimaeus.

That name is significant:
    it means,
    literally, "son of fear."
That's us, OK.
How often has fear stopped us,
    parked us alongside the road of life?
How often have we failed
    to go the extra mile with someone
    because we feared the involvement?
How often have we been silent,
    even with the person we're married to,
    because we were afraid?

This gospel writer understood fear
    and was writing to an audience
    that lived in fear of their very lives.
Only a few verses earlier,
    the gospel writer
    tells us a story
    about Jesus and the apostles.
They are talking among themselves,
    some of the apostles,
    about who would have glory
    in Jesus' kingdom.
    They're kind of dumb,
    those guys,
    because they don't understand
    the kind of kingdom Jesus was announcing.
So Jesus tells them,
"You don't know what you're talking about."
    "You must be *baptized*
      as I have been baptized,"
      he tells them,
    "and that baptism will render you a servant."

Servanthood,
> Jesus had tried to explain to them,
> involves giving up your life.

The apostles wanted a short cut to glory;
> they wanted to bypass
> the pain of death.

They feared the cost of being a follower of Jesus.

But getting back
> to poor old Bartimaeus.
> There he sat,
>> full of fear
>> stopped dead in his tracks
>> going nowhere
>> and wearing a heavy cloak.

And here we sit,
> afraid to turn in love to one another.

The very thing we want the most in life,
> to have real caring and loving
> is also the thing we fear the most.

The ache we feel deep inside us
> in our most honest moments,
> is the ache to be held,
>> emotionally and physically,
>> by someone who cares

and yet we refuse to allow that
> because the fear is so great.

But when Jesus came walking along,
> when he entered his life
> in the dramatic way that Jesus can,
> Bartimaeus realized that he had a chance
> and he began to cry out
> for all his worth!

"Jesus! Help me!"

And sure enough,
> Jesus heard his cry
> and called the old guy over to him.

Then the text says something interesting.

Bartimaeus, it says,
threw off his mantle.
He threw off the monkey on his back
the stone around his neck
the garbage he'd been carrying
that had weighed him down.
He threw off, in a word,
his fears,
and he came to Jesus.

What does this mean?
It means that he gave up his grip on himself
and came to realize that he
needed to be in Christ ,
which means he needed
that love and affection
we mentioned earlier.
Baptism is our entry into that,
but often it really is merely
a forgotten ritual
without lasting influence in our lives.
What it means to "reject Satan,"
what it means to be in Christ
is to reject isolation and aloneness
and accept community.
We do that,
accept community
by turning to one another
to share our lives together,
not in some safe, antiseptic way,
but in sharing:
intimacy
honesty
openness
kindness
and love.
In a word, we enter into Christ's community
when we take the real risk
of donating ourselves to one another.

So Bartimaeus threw off his mantle
    and went to Christ.
What did Christ say to him?
He asked him a question:
    "What do you want from me?" Jesus asked.
Baptism brings us to that question
    and, in fact,
    the baptism ritual of the church
    asks it of the unbaptized:
"What do you ask of the Church?"
    the ritual asks bluntly.

And what do you suppose Bartimaeus said
    to Jesus?
"I want to see," he said,
    "Please, I want to see."
I want to see what I am blind to.
    I want to see myself.
This text summarizes in a few brief lines
    what must have been quite
    a great relationship
    between Jesus and this man.
The gospels do that,
        but we can surmise from this
        that Jesus did help this man
        to see what he could not see
        because the story concludes
        by telling us that he was made well.
And then it tells us as well,
        that, once he'd received his sight,
        he was no longer parked,
            no longer stalled alongside the road.
The text is explicit in telling us
        that now he followed Jesus
        "on the way" down the road.

This is our story
        and it's the story of the baptized.
We're stopped short by our blindness,

by that inner condition
that renders us sinful sometimes.
But because of Christ,
with whom be begin to live at baptism,
we are made able to see,
we are restored to health,
we are made whole and, therefore, made holy.

The point of this story
is the point of our story:
We could cross the barren desert
without dying of thirst;
we could wander far in safety
without losing our way;
we could speak our words in foreign lands,
and all would understand:
we could see the face of God—*and live*!
We need not be afraid
to enter into our baptismal commitment.
We need not be afraid
to put on Christ by turning to one another.
We need not be afraid
because, although we suffer
an inner condition of weakness,
more powerful than that
will always be our inner condition of grace.

For Reflection and Discussion

1. What is original sin? (pp. 30–31)
2. What is the difference between being "unilateral" and being "relational"? (pp. 31–33)
3. What does it really mean to be baptized into a community/church? (pp. 35–38)
4. What keeps us from forming the bonds of real community? (pp. 38–42)
5. How can this parish make baptism more meaningful? What parts of the rite could be adapted to better fit our times?

Confirmation

We really haven't finished talking here
    about baptism.
In the church
    we finish talking about baptism
    when we talk
    about confirmation.
Confirmation finishes
    what baptism starts.

Our memories of our own confirmations
    might not be too clear,
    so let's start
    with a little refresher.
Many of us were confirmed
    only after we'd memorized a catechism
    full of answers.
The bishop would appear in our parish,
    which was usually enough
    to send the pastor
        into an absolute snit
    and the sisters
        into a frenzy.
(The confirmation ceremony was usually
    harder on them
    than it was on the students.)
Most of us were quite young
    when we were confirmed,
    maybe sixth grade or so.
Confirmation,
    we were taught,
    would make us soldiers of Christ,

and the slap from the bishop
was supposed to emphasize that.
But before any of that happened,
the confirmation or the slap,
we were warned by the sisters
that we would be drilled by the bishop.
We would all be seated
in the front pews of the church,
our nervous parents behind us,
and the bishop would stand
in front of us,
asking questions at random.
"Who made you?" he'd ask,
and then he'd glare at one of us
and we'd have to stammer to our feet
and blurt out an answer
or be killed later.
"Why did God make you?"
—the next question.
And, honestly,
at that moment,
it seemed that there might not
have been an adequate reason
for God to make me.
"God made me to know Him,
love Him,
and serve Him in this world,
and be happy with Him in the next,"
which seemed a good thing
because as we sat down in the pew again,
it was obvious
that we weren't very happy here.

They told us that if we couldn't answer
the questions,
we would be driven from the church
by the bishop,
disgraced before our parish and families
to be sealed in our perdition forever.

I doubt that bishops really did that very often,
    but the fear was enough
    to make us memorize those answers.
The only trouble was
    that they were answers to questions
        that we hadn't asked ourselves yet.
They were always someone else's questions,
    and, for most of us,
    that's where it's remained.

The approach under which most of us learned
    about our faith,
    as Bishop Raymond Lucker suggested,
    came from a belief
    that we could have information like this
    poured into our heads
        like milk poured into a pitcher.
If we could only get the facts straight,
    the reasoning went,
    we'd be strong in our faith.
And so we memorized and learned by rote.

Now, I don't doubt
    that it *is* important for us
    to know about our church.
We need the intellectual assent
    in order to give a strong commitment
    in faith.
But that surely isn't all there is to it.

We know today,
    and we try to help young people
    discover this today,
    that our faith is not in the church,
        or in the answers,
        or in the bishop.
Our faith is beyond that,
    in the Lord.
We experience God's grace

flowing through our lives,
touching our hearts,
sharing with others,
and being moved by the Spirit.
That grace flows from God,
with the church and its pastors
as hopeful agents of Christ's love.
We experience God,
not simply learn about God.
Discovering the experience of God in life
is as important as knowing
the formula of words to express belief.
Our faith, then,
does not lie in some particular way
of talking about God
but in a living and risen Lord
present within our everydayness.

There was a curious inconsistency
in the old system.
We were taught there about the Holy Spirit,
the Spirit of Truth,
who would reveal God to us.
We were taught there that
the Spirit of God
"blows where it wants to."
But that system itself
tended to prevent any real
freedom of the Spirit.
We didn't blow where the Spirit led us,
we blew where we were told to.
Under that system,
belief was static,
for the most part,
and believers were static, too.

But confirmation is about the Holy Spirit,
isn't it?
So, when the bishop demanded to know,

why did God make you?,
it could have been that
we had an opinion or two about that
        ourselves.
We may even have had some questions
        of our own to ask *him*.
But none of that mattered.
What mattered was that we could give
        the answer,
        his answer.
We know that the Holy Spirit
        has inspired the church
        to give right answers.
But we also know that *we* are that church.
The answers we bear in our hearts
        help form the answers that
        we write down in our catechism books.
The church is not static
        because we are the church,
        even when we are young and being confirmed.

We are the church,
        not set side by side unilaterally,
        alone together,
        but bound with the same breath,
        the same Spirit:
                a Holy Spirit.

For many of us,
        this Holy Spirit
        is the most shadowy member of the trinity.
I mean,
        God the Father—
        now that's a person
        you can really grab on to.
The symbol is so immediate:
        almost everyone has a father
        or a father figure in their lives.
We know, of course,

that God is not a father,
anymore than God is a mother.
Maleness is not a part of God;
no one would seriously argue otherwise.
But the whole father image
has been strong
and central for us.

Likewise the son image.
No one really has trouble
imagining what a son is like.
There are so many of them around
that it's easy to picture
what a son might look like.
It's easy to imagine Jesus,
a young male Jew of the first century,
roaming the backroads of the Holy Land
preaching and teaching
and eventually dying.
We know, of course, as Gene LaVerdiere has said,
that the risen Lord
is not a first-century male Jew.
Resurrection transcends maleness
and Jewishness
and first-century-ness.
But the whole image of being a son
is still an easy one
for us to grasp.

But the Spirit:
what's a spirit?
Just try to nail that one down
and see where it gets you!
A spirit is a breeze of wind,
a floating, hard-to-grasp notion
of God.

We did receive the Holy Spirit
at our own confirmations,
but few of us understood that,

and almost no one can talk about
what that means to them now.
It's an elusive,
      slippery,
      shadowy kind of thing.
But you will see in a moment here
      that it's also a central
            key
            necessary
            and altogether quite understandable
                  part of our lives.

Part of the problem in this
      is with the sign of the cross.
We line the three of them up there:
            Father
            Son
            Holy Spirit.
There is a theologically weak
      but very popular notion
      in lining them up this way,
      that God the Father is the most important
            of those three,
      followed by the Son,
      with the Spirit bringing up the rear.
It simply isn't true, though,
      that any of these is more important
      than another.
Really,
      practically speaking,
      it should be the other way around.
We should start by mentioning the Spirit
      because that is the most common experience
            of God.

Let's look at this a little closer here
      and see what this means.
These three ways of talking about God—
      Father, Son, Spirit—
      are really a way to describe

what *we* experience,
more than a way to describe God.
We don't know much about God
except what is revealed to us
in our own experience.
None of us has seen God,
as John points out,
so all we have to depend on
in talking about God
is our meager human experience.
So everything we say of God,
someone has observed,
is really a statement about ourselves.
We create a God image
that is really quite like our own.
We attribute to God
the characteristics we find in ourselves,
hoping somehow that we are like God
or that God is like us.

But God has also revealed God's self to us,
and we have learned to speak of this
as a three-part revelation.
This three-part form
which we call the Trinity
isn't simply a convenient way
to describe human experience,
though.
It is the way
we believe
that God has chosen and used
to reveal God's self to us.
But there is a certain
"poverty of speech,"
as St. Augustine has put it,
in trying to talk about these things.
We often run out of words to use;
we can't find an adequate way to
describe the reality of God.

If we could,
   would God really be God for us?
So when we speak of God as a person,
   or the Trinity as three persons,
   we have a "poverty of speech."

Is God a person?
Everyone knows that we don't mean to say
   that God is a person
   in just the same way that you and I
      are persons.
As persons,
   we are in a given time in history,
   and we live at a place on the planet.
We are a conscious center of initiative
   and experience.
We are persons like other persons.
And we have personalities:
   We're sometimes arbitrary
      capricious
      indecisive
      or changeable.

Those are all things that we can say
   about persons like ourselves;
   but when we say that God is a person,
   that's not what we mean.
So we have a poverty of speech.
We are humans and we have a human language
   that is for talking about human concerns.
The Godly concerns,
   which we are discussing here,
   can't be adequately described
   with plain words.

Because that's true,
   that plain words are too poor
   to describe and discuss God,
   we turn to another way of speaking:
      symbol.

To speak in symbolic words
  is to say only a little of what we mean,
  allowing the symbol we use
  to describe the rest
  in the deep unconscious of the mind.
The beauty of a symbol
  is that we don't have to say much about it.
For example,
  a Christmas tree.
You would never try to explain to someone
  what a Christmas tree means.
When you see one,
  anytime after Thanksgiving every year,
  something triggers within you,
  something bigger than words,
  bringing memories
    stories
    sensations
    emotions
    excitement
    wonder
    and even a song to our hearts.
It is a symbol of something so big,
  so tremendous,
  so ingrained within us,
    that we don't have to say anymore
    about it.
We just put up the tree.

Symbols work for us:
  they touch us
  move us
  and communicate to us
    when they are meaningful.
But sometimes symbols lose their meaning
  and become empty.

The words "God the Father"
  are symbolic words.

The human fathers that we all know
    are persons
    as we described persons earlier here:
        they live in a single place;
        they live in this century;
        they were born and will die;
        they can be arbitrary
           manipulated
           changeable
           and moody.

The words "God the Son"
    are symbolic words, too.
As we said earlier here,
    not all that is true of human sons
    is true of God the Son.
We use the words symbolically
    when we speak of sonship
    in reference to Jesus Christ.
The risen Lord
    is still the Son of God
    but not in the very same way
    that I am a son of my father.

The words "God the Holy Spirit"
    are symbolic words, as well.
We used to say
    Holy Ghost,
    referring to the image of ghosts
        as invisible
        but present beings.
Recently we began to say "spirit"
    instead of "ghost"
    in an attempt to improve the symbol,
    but there are still problems.
Is the Spirit a person?
We have a hard time understanding that,
    if it's true,
    because it doesn't seem to fit well.

Spirits to us aren't persons any more;
    they're sort of beyond being persons
    and live in a detached realm
    of which we know nothing.

In the first century,
    when these words were first used
    as symbols of God,
    the understanding of personhood
    was much less developed.
We live in a period of history
    with a much more
        psychologized understanding
        of human beings.
In the first century
    a rather unsophisticated time
    in terms of human understanding,
    the notion of personhood was
        much more mysterious
        than it is now.
There was much that was undiscovered
    in human psychology and medicine then.
They didn't know,
    for example,
    about the circulation of blood,
        psychological fixations,
        or even procreation.
A person was mysterious,
    which made the symbol of person
    a workable one in describing God.

But today we live in a highly psychologized,
    though, I suspect, still unsophisticated,
    time in history.
Today the notion of person
    as a symbol of God
    doesn't work very well.
Today that notion conjures up
    a science of understanding human nature

rather than a mysterious presence
of other beings living near us.
Today,
to speak of God as a person—
Father, Son, or Spirit—
results in that great poverty of speech
that we have been describing.

We want to return to that mystery
which the first century writers
sought in describing God.
We want to be able to talk about God
and allow our words to contain
a deep meaning
which allows God to be God.
We don't want to speak too surely
as though we know what we're talking about
and there can be no mistake about it.
We want, instead, to allow some room
in which we can grow in our understanding
and grow in our sensitivity to
God's presence.
The first century language,
because it was a less developed time,
was one that left this room for growth.
But our language about persons today
is laced with
a certain scientific understanding
which sounds too sure.
We still possess a poverty of speech;
but our new way of speaking of God
is at least a language for our time,
a language for today
and today's people.

Many of the changes we observe today
in people's understandings about God
and their practice of a religion
are due to this poverty of speech.

Remember that we're talking
    about confirmation as a sacrament
    or symbol
    of our life in God.
All of the points we are making here
    are essential
    if we are really to understand
        this sacrament.
How can we prepare for,
        celebrate,
            and receive the Holy Spirit
    if we do not first understand
    what that means today?

What can we say about the Trinity,
    and especially about the Spirit,
    in today's symbolic language?

In searching for a new symbol,
    something quickly emerges
        as a possibility: the symbol of "energy."
Though limited itself,
    this new symbol
    comes very close for us in this time,
    even though we know it may not be adequate
    for people in another time.
It comes from the work
    of Chardin
        Rahner
        Macquarrie
        and many others.
But principally
    it comes from the gospels.
It's an ancient symbol
    yet a thoroughly modern one.

We know only a little about energy,
    just as we know only a little about persons
    in the first century.

The more we learn about energy,
    the more we realize we don't know.
We understand,
    for example,
    that there is movement in energy,
        neutrons,
        photons,
        or whatever;
    but while it can be channeled,
    energy apparently cannot be created
        or destroyed.
It flows and empowers,
    energy does,
    but what is its source?
The sun, we would say,
    is the source of energy on earth,
    but what is the source of the sun?
And even within our own bodies,
    what is the energy that
    empowers our hearts to work continually
    for seventy, eighty, ninety, a hundred years?
And beyond the physical,
    what kind of energy is it
    that flows between lovers?
Where do ideas come from?
    Intuitions?
    Imaginings?
Where does the energy of life itself begin?
    Where death?

Without explaining too much more,
    let's begin to use the language
    of energy here
    to speak of the three-fold revelation
        of God.
Let's just see where this takes us.
This is a new way to talk about God.

There is a first experience of God

which in the past we have called
"God the Father."
With this new symbol
we would say that God is
the "generator" of life.
God is the Force
which is at the beginning
of all force.

What is the source of life?
Whence comes the energy of the earth
and its moon?
Who set the world on its axis?
Who provided for the first breath?
What is that generator
which produces the universe and
holds it together?
We have some sense of a source,
a force,
an author of life,
a father or mother,
giving birth to human life.
We experience, from time to time,
a deep, mysterious empowerment
within us
and among us.
We can know of human care
human energy
human strength and courage
human depth
which is not common.
We believe that beyond all of this,
beyond the deepest depth,
is the face of God.
We have not seen this face of God;
we only believe it is there.
But we have experienced its breath upon us
and its power within us.

We have known its presence
  because we have seen it in one another
  and especially in Jesus.

Jesus?
  The second experience of God
  which in the past we have called
  "God the Son":

Jesus: the expression of the unseen God;
  the Word of God;
  the ultimate sacrament of God;
  the only way many have ever seen
    or heard
    or touched
      God.

The second dimension of God that we can name,
  then,
  would be Word.

Words are full of energy:
  they create sound waves;
  they communicate ideas and dreams;
  and they can "enlighten" us
    when they are themselves
    the light of the world.
Words have a tremendous power
  to create or destroy us.
I remember watching a small black child
  on a school playground in Chicago
  one day.
Her friends,
  other black children,
  were pouncing on her and in doing so,
  they called her "nigger!"
As they did so,
  isolating her in a corner of the grounds,
  she hid in fear and shame.

A single word,
>> as Lenny Bruce has argued,
>> can destroy a person.
But only moments later,
>> one faithful childhood friend
>> had her arm around the wounded child
>> and re-created her
>> by calling her, simply, "friend!"

So God,
>> the Source of life,
>> expressed God's self to us in Word,
>>> in Christ.
This Word is so powerful
>> that it re-creates us.
It fills us with an energy of love
>> so profound
>> that we cannot live without it.
It is an energy of light,
>> the light of the world,
>> the burning bush,
>> the pillar in the night,
>> the light not placed beneath a bushel
>>> but set on high.
It is enlightenment and empowerment.
It is an energy,
>> as Paul said in giving his view of Christ
>> in Colossians,
>> an energy which holds the world together.

In a word, it is grace.

Grace is a power itself,
>> an energy from God
>> which enables us to become
>> all that we're created to be.

It is the grace of self-forgetfulness

the grace of caring
the grace of relational living.
And this grace,
we believe,
is an experience of the Holy Spirit.

The third way we experience God
in the past we have called
"God the Holy Spirit":

We said earlier
that we should begin
the sign of the cross
by naming the Holy Spirit,
rather than ending it there.
The Holy Spirit is the most common
experience of God.
That's why we call ourselves
"spiritual" when we're speaking
of our life in God.

One of the hallmarks of Karl Rahner's theology
is his notion that every human being
is united with God.
"To be," Rahner would say,
"is to be with God."
Even when we don't know it,
or even when we don't admit it,
still,
being oriented toward God
is a fundamental dimension
of being human.
As such, Rahner argues,
grace,
the grace of Christ,
is withheld from no one.
What is this grace?
It is the energy of self-awareness,
of growth,
of life itself.

It is the energy of breath
    knowledge
    truth
    beauty
    and goodness.
It is the energy of the
    Word of God
    expressed to us in Christ
    who promised us the Spirit of truth.
But over and above all of these,
    this grace is the energy of love itself,
    a grace denied to no one.

Thinking this over,
    it seems to make sense to us.
No human being is merely an animal.
Everyone has that special quality
    of self-reflection,
    of basic goodness,
    of orientation toward mystery
        that tells us we are graced.
Being graced, therefore,
    and being human
    are one and the same thing.
While this is true,
    it is also true that not everyone
    has met Jesus.
Fewer still, perhaps,
    have seen the face of God.
But everyone, it seems,
    everyone lives under the energy
    of the Holy Spirit.
Everyone is energized for life.

What is this experience of being energized
    this way?
What does it mean to be
    energized for life?
It means,

in a word,
that we become united
        to our real, full selves,
and that we become united
        to one another,
but more,
        that we become united
        with the Source of life itself.
The experience of God
        is an experience of unity.
It is a being related
        to ourselves and others,
        a "coming home" to self.

This level of unity,
        of relatedness,
        is one unavailable without the Spirit,
        without the experience of God.
It's a high level of unity,
        higher than would ever have been possible
        had not God as Source become
        expressive in Christ.
This is true because
        the revelation given us
        when God was expressed in Word
        through Christ
        is a revealing of us to ourselves.
"You will know the truth,"
        the gospel says,
        "and the truth will make you free."
The truth which makes us free
        is not an abstract
        theological truth known only to scholars.
No, it is a truth known in our very bones;
        it is a conrete, real,
        lived everyday kind of truth.
It is the truth about us;
        it is our truth.
When we know it, then we are free,

as the gospel promises,
but free for what?
Free, in short, to be our ownmost selves,
our very most real selves.
This self, we will find, when we are in Christ,
is never a self-for-self,
it is always a self-for-others,
and a self-for-God.
It is a self oriented to the deep mysteries
and realities of the divine Source.
It is a self flowing from that Source
and yet journeying toward it as well.

And this spirit
is the grace
of the sacrament of confirmation.

When the apostles and disciples
of the early church
first experienced the risen Christ
in their midst,
it was profound.
What does the text of the gospel
have to say about this?
In John's community,
it was written like this:
The followers of Jesus,
people just like us,
were pictured hidden behind locked doors.
They were said to be hiding there
in fear.

Isn't that just like us?
Aren't we often hiding in fear
of our own very selves?
Don't we fear the cost of being a disciple
of Christ?
Don't we hide ourselves,
afraid to come out

afraid, that if we do, we will
        be persecuted and maybe killed?
Don't we lock up our hearts
        from one another?
Don't we hide behind our role
        our money
        our beliefs
        our addictions
        our old habits
        our poor self-images?

So, anyway, there they were,
        hiding behind locked hearts
                (and doors).
Jesus' presence in their midst, however,
        carried a great power.
His presence in their lives,
        made mysterious now
                because of the resurrection,
                carried with it a great peace.

Receive peace, he told them,
        receive grace,
        receive divine power to live.
Receive yourselves;
        do not hide;
        be not afraid.
Receive me,
        receive a power to be
                your ownmost selves.
Receive the Holy Spirit
        and know that you have this power.
If you fail to forgive someone,
        then they will not be forgiven
        because forgiveness begins here—
                with you.
But if, in your goodness,
        you do forgive someone,
                then indeed they shall live!

This business of forgiveness of sins
    has often been misread here.
In the hierarchial days of the church,
    we took this literally to mean
    that our leaders had an arbitrary power
        to either forgive
        or refuse to forgive
            a penitent's sins.

But if we read this text
    within the context of this entire gospel,
    it much more likely
        points in another direction.
You have a great power,
    Jesus was saying here,
    to "make or break" each other
    in the spiritual life.
You can hear the words from another gospel
    echo here:
    Forgive us as we forgive others,
    and do not lead us to evil.
In other words,
    once we have received the Holy Spirit,
    we are not alone.
We interact with one another,
    and our attitude must be that
    of Christ.
We must take an unconditional regard
    for one another
    in order to help one another
    come to be the persons we are
        created to be.
If we do that,
    if we stop holding sins against each other,
    then we enable one another
    to grow,
        to overcome evil,
        to choose light and goodness.
But if we hold out against one another,

then we cause one another
to turn away.

Receiving the Holy Spirit
    renders us able to experience God
    as the revealer,
    the self-revealer who opens
        us unto our selves and others.
Receiving this Spirit
    renders us open to God,
    renders us desirous of God.
Receiving this Spirit
    renders us united to God,
    united to our own selves
    and united to our community,
        the church.

Confirmation is not a time
    when the Holy Spirit
    is dispensed for the first time.
We don't come to this sacrament
    to "receive" the Holy Spirit.
Rather, we come to this holy moment
    in order to celebrate in public
    our belief and our experience
    of being filled with the Holy Spirit.
It's a time to celebrate with family and friends
    a condition already present
    in the confirmand:
    that he or she is filled with holy life.

Some would say that this sacrament,
    confirmation,
    needs to be combined with baptism
    or done away with altogether.
Maybe instead
    we merely need to start taking it seriously,
    and along with it,
    the role and work of the Spirit,

which is the experience of God
in our lives.
When we prepare young people
to celebrate this sacrament, then,
we would help them first
come to grips with the divine power
of revelation in their lives.
This would mean that we could no longer
mass produce confirmation classes.
Each candidate would require pastoring
guidance
counsel
and support
as he or she would begin
tentatively
to allow themselves to be energized
by this divine power.
It would bring our young people
into a situation of facing themselves
with the loving acceptance
of a community to support them.
Then they could face our needy world
bring food to the hungry,
and change to the system
that makes people hungry.
And this would be how they come, in the end,
to face God in their lives.

This would require a real decision,
not a fake decision,
on the parts of the candidates,
a decision to know and accept themselves
to thereby "put on Christ like a garment,"
to believe in their own humanness,
to accept their own limits,
and, finally,
to enter into the dying
of the Paschal Mystery,
the ultimate expression of faith.

It would require of them that they ask,
    from their need,
    to be joined with the church
    in each one's journey to truth.

Permit me to dramatize this for a moment:
    picture a young person today,
    or for that matter, any of us,
    standing in a marketplace
        at the center of town.
Spinning madly about us are lights,
    dazzling lights, luring us toward them.
They are the lights of the market:
    the potential for more money,
    the whole sex industry,
    wily advertising agents,
    fast living,
    entertainment, food, drink, drugs.
We are tugged and pulled from every side.
It all looks so real;
    it all looks so satisfying;
    it all looks like so much fun!
But here we stand,
    spinning in the midst of this,
    wondering which to choose.
So first we choose this,
    then that,
    but nothing seems to satisfy.
Then off to one corner we notice a church,
    standing quietly by.
Its light is the light of the world,
    but we notice that its approach
    doesn't match the market very well.
It too calls us,
    but it asks much more.
It asks us to die in order to live,
    to give in order to receive,
    to risk ourselves instead of our money.
But we notice as well

that this church offers a glimpse
of the God who is with us,
rather than the false gods
we chase in the market.
How can we make it possible
for a young person to notice
before it's too late?
How can we make it possible
for us to see this community of believers,
who have found the real happiness?
How can this church
become home for our young people?
Confirmation is the sacrament of choice,
an adult decision,
and the beginning of a life of faith.
It is a time for young people
to choose to be themselves,
to live with us as church,
and to take on the work of God.
If we would take this sacrament seriously,
it could change the face of the church.
And then the Spirit would be sent forth,
the world would be re-created,
and this wonderful divine power
could renew the face of the earth.

For Reflection and Discussion

1. Describe God the Father, God the Son, God the Holy Spirit. (pp. 52–55)
2. How is "the Father" Creator? (p. 59)
3. How is "the Son" Word? (pp. 60–61)
4. How is "the Spirit" Truth? (pp. 62–65)
5. What does it mean in your life to be filled with the Holy Spirit? (pp. 65–71)
6. How can this parish make this sacrament more meaningful? What parts of the rite could be adapted to better fit our times?

Eucharist

At the last supper,
    when Jesus said,
    "This is my body,"
    he probably wasn't talking
        only about the bread.
He was talking about
    the community gathered there,
    about their love and care,
    about their being together again.
He was talking about
    himself,
    Christ present as teacher
        healer
        leader.
He was talking about
    sharing a meal in solidarity.
He was talking about all the sharing
    they'd done over the years,
    all the words they'd spoken,
    words of truth
        love
        kindness.
He was talking about *the* word,
    his word and theirs.
He was talking, in short,
    about his body,
    the body of Christ,
and he was also talking about the bread.

But the bread,
    by itself,
    separate from the community,

not shared in that moment,
not part of that gathering,
　　would be only bread.
What makes the bread sacred
　　is not a magical formula of words
　　but the reality of unconditional love.

So this meal wasn't just bread and wine.
　　No,
　　it was much more.
It was bread broken
　　and wine poured out.
It was a paschal life
　　and a paschal death.
It was a person's life given for others
　　and a new way of eating and drinking
　　that would last forever.

When we were kids growing up
　　in the church,
　　we were taught that there was
　　nothing more sacred than the host.
The host was everything to us;
　　it was that which we adored,
　　made double genuflections before,
　　received only after careful,
　　　　soulful scrutiny,
　　and knew we could never touch.
You weren't even supposed to look at it,
　　unless you bowed your head
　　and knelt, striking your breast.
In fact,
　　we couldn't even touch the chalice
　　that held the hosts.
The host was the bread
　　and the guest was Christ.

We were taught about this
　　before we could really understand it.

And we were taught by pious teachers
   who themselves had developed
   some strange beliefs
      about the bread
      and Christ's presence
      and how all this worked.
It's understandable that strange things
   would emerge.
   This belief is so central to our faith.
It is often true that we develop
   the largest set of customary beliefs
   about those things most important to us.
So we gradually picked up some ideas
   about how Christ was present and,
   depending on how much stress
   our pious teachers placed
   on the flesh of Christ,
      we may even have believed
      that chewing it
      hurt the Lord somehow.
We got this all mixed up.
   The mass, we were made to understand,
   was the unbloody re-enactment
      of Christ's bloody sacrifice
      on the cross.
What happened at Mass was intensely personal
   between Jesus and me.
The notion of a shared moment,
   a holy moment of unity,
   was absent for the most part.

A whole host of questions
   then gathered for us:
Did we re-crucify Christ
   through his bread?
      Would he bleed again?
   And what about the wine:
      how could you have the body of Christ
      without the blood, too?

Was this bread really the physical flesh
of Jesus Christ,
the first-century male Jew?
Or was it some greater reality
having to do with the body
of the risen Lord?
We weren't really sure
and maybe we still aren't.
The one thing we did know
was that Christ in the bread
was "up there,"
on the other side of that communion rail,
and we were all "down here,"
on our side.
We were taught, above all, to be reverent
whenever we were in the presence
of the host.

The stress was on reverence:
don't talk or even walk
in the presence of the host;
make a double genuflection
anytime you move within sight
of the host;
don't think about anything but God
when you're in church;
fold your hands when you walk back
to your pew from communion
and point them toward heaven;
kneel down and close your eyes.

I really don't think that this was reverence
for the eucharist.
I think it was a scrupulosity
founded in an exclusive focus
on the bread at Mass.
And this came from a too literal
interpretation of what Jesus meant

when he said,
"This is my body."

It is never appropriate for us
    to take one word or line
    from the gospel
    and decide that it is literally true
        while the rest is not.
We must take a consistent approach
    to understanding the gospel;
    and we must, in a sense,
    take each phrase as a part of the whole.
We cannot be literalists à la carte.

The phrase, "This is my body,"
    taken as part of the whole gospel,
    could not possibly be a reference
        only to bread.
The body of Christ
    for Jesus and the early followers
    was clearly the community of God.
Each time a reference is made to the body
    and its parts,
    it is a reference not to bread
        but to people.
Even at the Lord's Supper itself
    it isn't simply bread,
    it is bread *broken*.
It isn't just wine,
    it is wine *poured out*!

So our reverence must be,
    not simply for bread,
    but for bread broken,
        shared,
        inclusive of all,
        the body of Christ,
        us, them, everyone.

All this business of
    not looking at,
        touching,
        standing in the presence of,
        and generally being in awe over the bread
    must be translated today
    into a profound acceptance
        of the community,
            both gathered
            and absent.
We do need to be reverent,
    but our reverence must be
    for the body of Christ:
        for the poor
        those on the streets
        those excluded by our norms
        the dirty
        the hungry
        for children in poverty
        for the poor wealthy.
In a word,
    we must hold in reverence
        the tax collector
        prostitute
        and public sinner.
Then we will have held in reverence
    the body of Christ.
Then the real presence of Christ
    in the eucharistic bread
    is worshipped and honored.
Then we will have washed each other's feet.

When we receive communion
    and the distributor says
    "The body of Christ,"
he or she is saying, really,
    "Do you accept the body of Christ,
        the community here,
        these people
            with their weaknesses

their sins
their differences from you?"
"Do you accept this body,
and will you heal it
feed it
care for it
and cherish this body?"
"Do you accept the body of Christ?"
And when we answer "Amen,"
we are likewise saying "Yes."
"Yes, I do accept the responsibility
of living in the body of Christ.
"Yes, these are my sisters and brothers
and so are those others,
all of them."
"I do accept the body of Christ."

I can't help but recall that great story
from the Gospel of John
where Jesus and those fisher men and women
were having breakfast
on the beach.
The story doesn't open
with the breakfast scene, though.
It opens with the supper,
which, in John's account of this,
was almost entirely
the story of Jesus washing their feet.
It was the story of a love affair
so deep and so profound
that there wasn't anything
that was too much.
There wasn't anything he wouldn't do
for them
and they for each other and him.
The intimacy of bathing together,
of washing one another,
of tenderness and affection,
physical affection,
expressed in a touching scene.

We shouldn't be surprised to see this.
The central point of Jesus' message,
>after all,
>>was that we should love one another.
We often think of this command to love
>when we think of gospel love,
>>as a sort of antiseptic
>>>sexless
>>>emotionless
>>>touchless
>>>"clean" kind of love.
I really think this misses the boat completely
>and is a leftover
>from an age where we were taught
>not to love our bodies.
We were taught that they were earthy,
>>part of "this world,"
>>and not spiritual.
We were taught that sex is impure,
>that we shouldn't touch one another,
>and that expressing affection
>>is not necessary
>>and certainly not holy.
In short,
>we have been taught
>that the body
>>is not a good thing.

But if the incarnation means anything,
>it means that the body *is* good,
>just as it was declared good
>>at the time of creation.
If John is insistent about anything,
>it is that Jesus came in the flesh.
We have sometimes so spiritualized
>our faith in him
>that it doesn't seem to matter
>>that Jesus was in the flesh.
We find it oddly easier to believe
>in Jesus' divinity

than we do his humanity,
    "which we have seen with our own eyes."
Both the creation and the incarnation
    insist that earth is good,
        that flesh is good
        that we are good.
Flesh and love are deeply intertwined
    with one another;
        that's the great joy of being human.
But our over-spiritualization of religion
    has turned this around
    and made us believe that flesh
        is somehow bad.
What often happens in this turned-around state
    is that love no longer
    holds a place of importance for us.
The only important thing is to be right.

But God is not found in theology,
    nor a moral code,
    nor a religion.
God is found in the centerpoint
    of John's gospel:
        Love
God is found in flesh,
    according to the Incarnation;
    and our call is not to be right,
    but to love.

We prefer to think of Jesus
    and his friends
    as people who did not even have bodies,
    much less use them in their
    loving presence to one another.
We have institutionalized this
    as a church,
    in setting up as holy
    those who do not have sex.
We want priests and ministers,

sisters and brothers,
who are sexless
emotionless
touchless
and "clean."
This is what we've told ourselves:
people who do not
express intimate physical affection
are holier than those who do.
We've got this backwards;
that was the point of the gospel.

This denial of the physical reality
of the body,
and its place in our loving
is at the core
of the liturgical crisis we face
with the eucharist today.
This is at the core
of the sterile,
automated liturgical form
which dominates in the church.
This is at the core
of the often dead crowds,
the often small crowds
and the often bored crowds
who show up on Sundays.
I mean,
we come for eucharist
to express community and love
as Christians.
How do we do that?
We line up in pews,
everyone facing no one,
everyone touching no one;
and we sing together,
but we try not to interact
with anyone else
because that might be embarrassing.

We express our gospel love,
    we are told when we get there,
    by simply being there (!)
    by singing along with all the verses (!)
    and by giving generously
        at the collection (!).
The eucharist itself,
    the sharing of the bread
    is equally antiseptic.
We use a kind of non-bread,
    a wafer which meets only a minimal
    definition of bread.
In some dioceses
    there's more concern with the recipe
    for this wafer
    than with the quality of the gathering.
I'm not sure why we don't use real bread.
Maybe it's because then
    what we do might resemble,
    (God forbid!),
    the Lord's Supper.

Lord help us!
    It's no wonder that the eucharist
    is not the center of life for very many.

Let's go back,
    though,
    to that bunch of Jesus' friends
    who shared this meal together.

They ate and drank together often
    because they loved to be together.
And on this particular night,
    their eating and drinking
    was special;
        something was in the air.
Have you ever had a dinner party,
    or been to one,

with your family,
    maybe just the two of you
      out for a special night,
    maybe a holiday or birthday,
    maybe just good friends,
      gathered together in love?
A dinner party that went on and on...
    ...being together,
      talking about important things
      as well as trivial things,
    ...being together,
      cooking, serving, laughing, singing
    ...being together,
      a long pre-dinner time,
      then the meal, slow and comfortable,
      wine, good food,
        better because it's shared,
      then linger over coffee
      and when you thought
        there couldn't be anything else,
      out comes the dessert!
But wait! We're not done yet.
    Then there's the afterglow,
    maybe in front of a fire,
      or sitting on the porch,
      sipping a coridal or a coffee.

And even then it isn't over
    because you know
    that the next time you are together,
    you will remember this meal,
    and you will talk about it.
You will say how wonderful it was
      and how this or that
      really touched you.
It'll be almost like enjoying it
    all over again.

That's the dinner party
    we're talking about here.

It wasn't like the ones we would have today
    but it was a first century equivalent.
And it was in this context
    that we see Jesus
    at the end of the evening,
    get up from that table,
    and spend time with each person there,
        washing their feet
        kissing their feet
        anointing their feet.
Here was an expression of love
    so profound
    that we cannot even imagine it.

If there is a holy moment in Jesus' life
    to which we can point and say,
    "This is when he founded the church,
    this is when he instituted the sacraments,"
        it was when he washed their feet.
We keep looking through the Scriptures
    looking for a time
    when Jesus might have given
    his followers some new authority
    and we want to point to that
        and call it
        the founding of the church.
But read carefully:
    it was when he washed their feet
    that he founded this church.

This is the apostles' real baptism;
    this is their healing
    their reconciliation
    their call to ministry.
This is, most importantly,
    their eucharist.
This is, for John and for us,
    the moment where the body of Christ
    is embraced,

shared,
broken.
This intimate love-making among them
    replaces for John
    any words of institution.
The line,
    "This is my body,"
    is omitted in this gospel.
The only reference
    is to this body of Christ
    in love and service.

But after dinner,
    after the love-making of that moment,
    they'd run away from him
    before he got to the trial.
They feared that they, too,
    would be killed,
    that what was demanded of Jesus
    would also be demanded of them.
They ran off,
    leaving their close friend alone;
    they were
        frightened
        alone
        depressed
        and confused.
In leaving Jesus,
    they also left each other
    and their own very selves.
How could they have stayed together?
    Someone might notice them gathering.
    Someone might remember
        that they were with Jesus.
    Someone might have accused them
        of being part of that crowd.
Someone actually did that to Peter,
    waiting in front of that charcoal fire
    in the courtyard.

So they split up,
    some going here,
    some going there.
They may have run off into the small towns
    and villages near Jerusalem.
They may have hid in their homes,
    or the homes of friends.
We don't know where they went to hide,
    but we do know that they hid.

It's almost impossible to know
    in your heart
    what this would have been like
      for them
      unless you have yourself
    been part of a friendship like theirs.
We know from the gospels
    that these people
    were not theologians.
They barely understood what Jesus was saying
    most of the time.
We know that they weren't
    great community leaders
    in their day.
They were pictured by some of the writers
    of the testament
    to be dunderheads,
      slow to understand
      slow to accept
      slow to get it all straight.

But these people lived with Jesus
    and each other
    in a way that created a bond
    of love and friendship
    which ran deep in their being
    and which became the center of their lives.
Have you ever lived with a friend
    or a group of friends

or a spouse
or children
whom you really loved?
Do you know the joy of hearing
a voice you recognize
in the morning
or on the phone
or in the hallway
or at the table?
Do you know the sound of your name
when it's called by someone you love?
Do you know the tremendous sense
of security and well-being
that comes from that loving friend?
There are no words to describe
what I'm pointing to here,
and I'm doing a poor job
of trying.

But if you are a person
who does not know and understand
the love of which I speak,
then you cannot possibly
understand the eucharist
on any level except the intellectual.
Eucharist is a sacrament of the heart
as well as the body.

So these people who'd been with Jesus
in this wonderful loving friendship
were now without him completely.
He'd been carted off
and they'd fled in fear.
They were isolated,
distant from one another,
without anyone to share;
in a word,
they were without love.
It was a time of darkness for them all.

Who knows how long they were alone?
The text tells us
    that they had gathered again
    on the third day
    but we know that the number three
        is a special scriptural number
        which means, really,
        "in due time..."
So it may have been three days,
    or three weeks,
    or even longer.
We just don't know.

The point here isn't the number of days,
    but that they did finally
    begin to gather again.

Slowly they began to reconnect,
    one by one they found one another again,
    as their nerve returned,
    and they came back into public.
Gene LaVerdiere paints a picture
    of them meeting in the market,
    maybe at one another's homes.
After the death of Jesus,
    they may have made plans
    to go back to their former ways of life.

Eventually,
    as this story in John's gospel tells it,
    they gathered at the sea.
That would've been the natural place
    to look for them
    because that's where many of them
    had started with Jesus.
So there they sat on the shore,
    gathered in the darkness
    because they were still in fear.
But at least they were together,
    which was better than being alone.

As they talked and fished through the night,
    something began to happen among them.
They may have finally been admitting
    their denial of him
    and of themselves.
They may have finally been sharing
    their fears,
        sorrows,
        angers,
        and loneliness.
As they fished that night,
    we know they had plenty of time to talk
    because they weren't catching any fish.
"Boat talk" is the kind that lingers for us,
    it floats above the water
    it is easy,
        honest,
        profound,
        and intimate.
It's like pillow talk,
    or riding-in-the-car talk
    or doing-the-dishes talk
    or going-for-a-walk talk.
And as they talked,
    they began to feel that solidarity again,
    that sensitivity to one another,
    that brother and sisterhood
        that they'd known with Jesus so often.
They began to feel his presence again,
    to know his power
        his love,
        his words.
It was a time of reconciliation for them,
    a coming home to each other
    and to their own very selves.

Maybe they even began to tell
    his stories again,
    when he did this or said that.

And finally,
> the text says,
>> as the dawn was breaking over their lives
>> and the morning of that day,
and as they gathered to share a meal,
> they realized that he was still with them,
> that his powerful presence had not ended,
>> but had only changed.
It was in that moment,
> as the gospel writer tells this story,
> that we gain an insight
> into the eucharist
> that changes our lives.

For it was in that context
> that we recall the words of Jesus
> to Peter:
If you really love me,
> Jesus said,
>> and you want to share this meal with me,
>> then you must care for my lambs,
>>> which is the whole body of Christ.
If you come to this meal
> and ask to be in this community of God,
> then you must feed my sheep,
>> which is the whole body of Christ.
If you come to the eucharist,
> Paul had earlier written,
> and you have not made peace in your life
>> with the people around you,
>> then go and do that first.
If you come to the eucharist
> and some haven't been fed,
> then see to it that they are fed first.
If you come to the eucharist
> and there still remain divisions among you,
> then your eucharist does harm,
>> not good
> and in fact, Paul wrote,

when that is true, it isn't the eucharist
at all!

In the church today,
we have found convenient ways
to understand this
that do not hurt very much.
We have remembered the bread,
but forgotten the body of Christ.

But what does this mean for our age
and for the future of our church?
We often count the sacraments
as though they are all equal.
They aren't.
Some are more central in life
and in the church
than others.
Eucharist is the most central.

But we attend mass so often
and we receive eucharist so frequently,
that it has lost its punch.
Coming to Mass,
we expect,
should make us feel good.
It should be a hushed time
of music,
candlelight,
incense,
and warmth.
We want to wear our best clothes,
our "Sunday best,"
and we treat it all
like a great social event.

But in truth,
this should be
the single most disturbing moment
of the week for us.

Have we interrupted the power
   of this sacrament
   to make Christ "really present"
   by so compromising
      our celebrations
      that they are meaningless?

It was people receiving the eucharist,
   we must remember,
   who exterminated six million Jews,
      homosexuals
      mentally and physically handicapped
      and others judged to be inferior.

It was people receiving the eucharist,
   we must remember,
   who incinerated two Japanese cities,
      men, women, and children,
      with a nuclear weapon.

It is people receiving the eucharist,
   we must remember,
   who systematically imprison our poor
      in poverty ghettos,
      while building mansions for themselves.

It is people receiving the eucharist,
   we must remember,
   who are building an arsenal of weapons
      that may destroy the earth
      and who are doing it
         in the name of "peace."

It is people receiving the eucharist,
   we must remember,
   who kill one another in Ireland,
   who maintain apartheid in South Africa,
   who fund rightwing death squads
      through the CIA in Central America,

who sell weapons in the whole world,
    and who have impoverished the third world
        by exporting its resources
        to live in wealth.

It is we who receive the eucharist,
    we must remember,
    who continue to live in our narrow worlds,
    who continue to murder in our streets,
    who continue to abuse our children,
    who continue to hoard,
        lie,
        steal,
        and hurt others.

What does eucharist mean for us today?

Of course,
    the eucharist itself is powerful
    and there are others who receive it as well:
        Martin Luther King, Jr.
        Dorothy Day
        Oscar Romero
        Jean Donovan
        Thomas Merton
        Mother Teresa
    and many like them.
And then there's us:
    we who come on Sunday
    hoping for a breakthrough this week.
We are there, too,
    and most of us aren't terribly evil
        or terribly good.
Nonetheless, this is the holy moment
    in the week
    that can make peace,
        establish justice,
        and pull us toward wholeness.

We find ourselves
    both ready to embrace the body of Christ
    and still too sinful to look up.
We are a mixture,
    on our way, but not there.

Church documents rightly remind us
    that eucharist is to be
    both the source of our life in faith
        as well as its ultimate end.
But have we made a mockery of our gathering
    by maintaining a Sunday "celebration"
    that comforts people in their
    status quo?

I would like to endorse here
    those eucharists that give us
    a wonderful glowing feeling.
But I can no longer do so.
More than any other moment in our week,
    that moment when we are confronted
    by the body of Christ,
    assembled and absent,
    represented and present in the bread,
        is a moment of challenge,
        not of mushy feelings.
Am I too harsh, too demanding here?

I hope not,
    but there is a question which haunts me
    concerning the majority of the people
        on this planet:
            the ones who suffer
            hunger
            and thirst;

            those imprisoned
            killed
            and tortured;

those excluded
ridiculed
abused
and mistreated:

Who will wash their feet today?
Who will be willing to pay that awful price?

For Reflection and Discussion
1. What is the Body of Christ? (pp. 72–78)
2. What does the birth of Jesus as a human being with a body mean for us? (pp. 78–82)
3. How can we wash one another's feet in our community? (pp. 82–85)
4. What does it mean for you to receive the Body of Christ? (pp. 91–95)
5. How can your parish make this more real? What parts of the rite could be adapted to better fit our times.

Reconciliation

When he was away from home
    in that foreign country
    where he'd spent his father's money
    on loose living and other unholy things,
    the prodigal son,
        the text of Luke says,
        "came to himself..."

Augustine had that experience
    in just as dramatic a way
    as this father's son.
"You were right before me," he wrote
    in his *Confessions*,
    "but I had moved away from myself.
        I could not find myself;
        how much less, then,
            could I find you?"

Grace, we have said elsewhere,
    is when God communicates God's self to us
    by revealing us to ourselves.
This grace is made available to us
    by God alone.
No one else created us,
    no one else has made us whole
        provided healing
        given us a salve
        given us salvation.
To be away from oneself
    is to be away from this revelation,
        this healing,
        this saving presence of God.

It is, in short, to be away from grace.

This being-away-from-oneself
     that the gospel writer
     and Augustine have described,
   this having-left-our-home,
   this inner condition,
     is sin.

To reconcile that
     is to bring oneself back together,
     as it were.
It is a restoring of the created order,
     an undoing of Adam and Eve's sin
     a coming home to oneself
     a coming home, period.
And all of this
     coming and going
     is done with the incredible intimacy
     of God's deep love.
"The ultimate purpose of penance,"
     Paul VI once wrote,
     is that we should "love God deeply
     and commit ourselves completely to him."

"Come back to me with all your heart,"
     the Lord calls,
     "with all your heart...."

This sacrament,
     called sometimes penance
     sometimes reconciliation
     popularly called confession
       this sacrament
is a standing naked before God,
     a spiritual and emotional nakedness
     and sometimes a physical nakedness,
     which renders us able
       to be completely honest

to hide nothing
to receive God's love
        even when we are away from
        and do not love ourselves.
It is when we are naked
    that we are most vulnerable,
    but not until then can we
        experience deep, profound love.
This sacrament brings us out of hiding;
    it brings us
    and our deeds
        into the light
        and does so with force.

It takes us to the deepest recesses
    of our being
    where we find that
    the heart of the Lord is mercy.
But, and here's the pith of our problem,
    the journey to the heart of the Lord
    is never travelled alone.
We go there together
    and only together.
We are a people,
    not set side by side collectively,
        as someone has written,
    but bound together
    united by the Holy Spirit.
And this is the problem for us:
    reconciliation means we have to deal
    with people.
Reconciliation done in secret
    is not really reconciliation at all.
We cannot be intimate alone.

Whatever rite we use to celebrate
    this great news
    must reflect the many realities
        of the sacrament.

It must provide for intimacy,
    not simply give the "news."
It must encourage us
    support us
    sustain us
    bring us home.
And it must bring us together,
    finally,
    where we belong.
It must do this because,
    whatever else we say about reconciliation,
    the key is that we are called to it
        by God.
It's not simply something
    we may choose or not choose to do.
The call is written in our hearts;
    it is in our very bones.
The rituals of the church
    must serve this call;
    we cannot allow them to become absolute
        in themselves.
When the rituals are not working,
    then the rituals must be examined.

For many people,
    the rite of private confession
    is something they do not choose anymore.
Are these people wrong?
Or are they responding to something
    within themselves,
    prompting them to seek reconciliation
        in other ways?
Most people just don't talk about it,
    but I think that
    we need to have a frank little visit
    about sin and reconciliation.
Too many people,
    honestly admitting
    that confession to the priest

has not been sufficient,
have not been facing themselves,
     have been away from themselves,
     and, therefore,
          are away from God.

One of the reasons
     we need to have this little talk about sin
     is our memories.
Sin was a major aspect
     of the church in which
     many of us were raised.
It formed a reason
     for the first sacramental experience
     of our little lives:
     baptism.
We were born,
     we were told,
     in original sin which baptism
          removed from our souls.
Then before we received our
     first communion,
     even as little kids,
     seven, eight years old,
     we were taught to examine ourselves
     for serious, mortal sins.
We were searching our young hearts
     for ways that we'd rejected God,
     and chosen Satan.
We were so young that we were barely capable
     of making a choice of that magnitude,
          of really rejecting God,
          but search we did
          under the always watchful eye
          of our catechism teachers.
We lived, then, with the constant fear of hell.
We knew that the failure
     to confess
     even one mortal sin
     would seal us in hell forever.

We knew that some of the sins
    we were looking for
    were hidden sins
    in a category known as omission.
These were the kind that
    you didn't even know you were committing.
We memorized perfect acts of contrition
    and frequently went to confession
    all in an effort to keep our souls
    from the fire of hell.
"Oh, my God,"
    the act of contrition went,
"I'm heartily sorry for having offended thee,
    and I detest all my sins
    because I dread the loss of heaven
    and the pain of hell...."
There were certain unmentionable sins
    that were so evil
    they couldn't even *be* forgiven,
    not even by a bishop!
I think they were unmentionable
    because they really didn't exist.
Or it may have been that they
    were sins against purity
    which our pious teachers
        would not want to talk about
        because they would run the terrible risk
        of themselves having an impure thought
        and entering into concupiscence.
Whatever the case,
    I grew up with the awful tension
    within my young Catholic heart
    that I may,
        accidentally,
        have committed one of these sins.

We grew in time to really dread confession.
It stands out in many Catholic memories
    as among the worst of moments
    rather than the holiest.

One of the most anxious moments
    of my Catholic childhood
    was that one in which the bishop
    stood before our confirmation class
    and drilled us with questions.
I was filled with fear
    and I honestly think I had a blackout
    because I can't remember
    whether he actually asked me anything
        or not.
It was a horrible moment
    but at least it was over
    in fifteen minutes.
Confession went on and on and on...

We need to chat about this
    and now's the time.
We're going to talk about three aspects
    of sin.
First, we'll
    look at private sin,
    if there really is any such thing.
When we were being taught about sin,
    we were told that no sin
    is a purely private sin,
    that every sin we commit affects others.
I'm sure that's true,
    but some sins do seem
    more private than others.

In contrast, for example, to private sin
    is what we'll call social sin.
By this we will mean
    the stuff bigger than ourselves
    like failing to feed the starving millions
    forgetting to visit prisons
    ignoring the homeless
    building bombs to blow up the world
        and so forth.

The third kind of sin we'll talk about
    is public sin.
We have more public sinners,
    I think, than we used to have.
At least, people are more open
    about what we might call
    "lifestyle disobedience":
        divorce and remarriage
        gay and lesbian partnerships
        living together without marriage
        not going to Mass anymore
        and so forth.
I'm not sure that these folks
    are really sinners,
    in the strict sense,
    but they are often perceived to be,
    and that's why we'll call them that.

Once we've had a chance to look at those
    we can go ahead
    and chat about confession
        or reconciliation
        or penance
        or whatever we call it today.

We'll begin here
    by talking a bit
    about "private sin"
    that formed the bulk of our list
    in the old days
    when we made lists for confession.
The focus of piety in those days
    was on sin
    as an offense against the law of God.
The ten commandments of Moses
    formed the backdrop
    against which we examined ourselves
    each time we went to confession.
The law of Moses

was our guide,
rather than the mercy of Christ.
We searched our hearts
in the examination of conscience
in order to know how we had
broken the law.
We became scrupulous about that law.

There were, for example,
in my home,
great debates about what exactly
constituted "servile" work
on Sunday.
We were farmers
and this was a gray area for us.
Doing the routine and necessary chores
was always acceptable.
After all,
the argument went,
"If an ox or an ass," to quote Jesus,
"fell into a well,
would you not pull it out on the Sabbath?"
I never quite understood this argument
when I was a kid
because we didn't have an ox or an ass
and yet we still worked on Sundays.

Anyway, the chores were OK,
but what about baling hay on Sunday?
The answer to that was tougher:
if we needed the crop to ensure our
financial security,
and if we could see rain in the western sky,
then we could bale.
But if the forecast was for clear skies
and we were rich enough without it,
then we did not.
Thankfully, my wise parents
were always able to deal with this question,

and they followed their own
well-formed consciences,
    which, in the end,
    was what they were supposed to do anyway.
The kids in the family always argued
    to enforce this law literally:
        No work on Sunday!
    While my parents,
    who knew what needed to be done
        and what didn't,
    were more open to a flexible interpretation
    of this particular law.
So one way or the other
    we found our path
    among the thorns and thickets of the law.

But didn't all of this miss the point?
Wasn't the law's own demand
    that we *keep holy* the Sabbath?
Didn't this "servile work" approach
    tend to demean work as not holy?
Wouldn't it be possible to lie around all day
    and still not keep holy the Sabbath?

Let's talk about another area
    that was buried in the law: sex.
There were probably more rules about sex
    than any other single area
    of human activity,
    including keeping holy the Sabbath.
Let's just take one area of this law
    and see where it takes us.
Let's talk about sex within marriage.

According to the law,
    sex within marriage is acceptable.
So two married people can go ahead and have sex
    anytime they want.
True or false?

What about when one partner uses sex
        to manipulate the other?
What about when one uses it
        to control and dominate the other,
        demanding sex unilaterally
        "because it's my right"?
What about the common situation in marriage
        where the relationship between
        the two people has broken down
            or been ruptured
            or destroyed?
Can married people who no longer love each other
        have sex?

I think we can begin to see before us
        the difficulties of following a law
        that is not written upon our hearts.
The answers to these questions,
        whether or not to work on Sunday
        and whether or not to have sex
            within marriage,
        are simply not that clear.
The law
        does not necessarily help that much here
        because the law is too clear.
It makes it sound so simple.

But do you see?
It was the law on which we based
        our own early training as Christians.
When we went into that
        confessional box
        and knelt down in the darkness
        to report our list of sins,
        it was only the law,
            the law of Moses,
            on which we were reporting!
We may well have been angry
        with our brother or sister,
        but was that anger a healthy response?

Did it rise out of love,
    maybe even a tough love?

We may well have missed our daily prayers
    but were we suffering
    through a desert period of our life?
Were we in one of those times
    of darkness,
    a dark night for our soul?
Did prayer become difficult
    because we were wrestling with
    a larger issue of fidelity to God?

We may well have lied,
    but what in our own self-image
    was so repulsive to us
    that we would lie to hide it?
What about ourselves
    were we not facing
    that this lie could help us detect?

We may well have been guilty of greed,
    but what did our hoarding of wealth
    tell us about ourselves?
Were we lonely?
Did the greed replace love in our lives?
Had we wandered into a spiral of living
    wherein we needed ever more money
    in order to be happy now?
Had money become our god?

We may well have had that impure thought
    and allowed it to linger for a moment,
    but is sex dirty?
Was this sexual urge really "impure"?
Did it tell us something about our needs?
    about our own sexual self?

When I hear people asking

to return to the good old days
when we knew what was a sin
    and what wasn't,
        I think about these questions.

Then there is this whole new area of sin,
    one that we seldom confessed to
    in the box: social sin.
What about our failure to feed the hungry?
    How many of us confessed to that?
What about racism?
    sexism?
    consumerism?
    homophobia?
How about rampant militarism?
    Is it a sin to pay taxes that are used
    to build more nuclear bombs?
I think it may well be.

What's going on here?
This can all be just too confusing,
        can't it?
The clear lines that we used to draw
        between what is a sin
        and what is not
        seem lost forever.
Today we stand in the midst
        of a complex moral environment,
        with new global dimensions
        brought to us by television
        and we struggle, often very much alone,
            to know what to do.
For many of us,
        this struggle has paralyzed us,
        and I believe that so many of us
        have stopped going to confession regularly
            more because of this moral maze
            than for any other reason.

I remember sitting in my living room
    one evening not that long ago eating my dinner
    and watching a newscast
        on public television.
I recall now that I was eating
    leftover chicken and dumplings
    from a dinner party the evening before.
I had poured a glass of white wine,
    which was also a leftover,
    and it stood on my coffee table.
I was warm and comfortable,
    and even my leftovers tasted good
    at the end of a day of labor.
But on the news that night
    were some of the first pictures and stories
    from the deserts of Africa.
Here were these Ethiopians,
    women, men, and children,
    who hadn't eaten for days,
        maybe for weeks.
They were lined up at a food distribution center,
    begging for enough to get through the night.
They looked awful:
    thin
    worn
    sad
    starving.
I remember thinking,
        "Here they are,
        the starving millions!"
There they were
    and here I was.
    How could I eat?
    How could I live in such comfort?
    Were these people my responsibility?

I thought that evening that maybe
    I should confess eating dinner.
What would the priest say

if I came to confession and said,
    "Father, I ate my dinner...."
He'd think I was off my rocker.
But it suddenly seemed like a sin to me
    to be that well fed and comfortable
    with these people and the words of Jesus
    confronting me:
        "When I was hungry,
        you gave me to eat...."

But I felt confused as well
    because I remembered a line from
    George Gilder's *Wealth and Poverty,*
    the bible of supply-side economics,
    in which he argued that
    it is usually immoral to feed the poor.
"The poor," he said, "need the spur
    of their poverty
    in order to escape it."

Which was true:
    the literal gospel message
    or George Gilder's modern interpretation
        of that gospel?

There are many other complex moral questions
    which all of us face today.
It would be more tolerable for us
    if the causes of and the cures for
    these tough social problems
    were apparent,
    but they are not.
Differing points of view on this
    compete for our hearts and minds.
We live in a complex global environment
    in which sin is not so clear
    today.
It never will be again.

This lack of clarity
    and this complex moral environment
    have caused many of us
    to give up.
We can't figure it out,
    and we can't go on with this guilt,
    and we can't get answers anywhere,
    so we sink down before our televisions
        and try to forget it
        if we can.

The trouble is we can't.

Another complexity which we face today
    in sorting through
    questions of sinfulness is
    the growing number of public sinners
    we know.
I know a public sinner.

He sort of left the church during college
    and never really got back to it.
No one officially leaves the church,
    of course.
I mean, he didn't get un-baptized or anything;
    he just stopped attending Mass
    and obeying the rules.
Does that mean that he left the church?
    I'm not sure.
But he did miss Mass on Sunday numerous times
    and each time was a mortal sin,
    and he did it in public,
    so he's a public sinner, right?

Then when he got married
    it was to someone previously married,
    and divorced
    but without an annulment.
Another public sin.

Besides that, they lived together
    before they got married in the first place;
    cohabitation we call it:
    public sin number three.

There were probably other public sins,
    but three seems like enough
    for me to make my point.
You should meet this guy!
    He's a great guy,
    and his wife's a super gal!
    And so are their kids!
Are their souls in darkness
    and are they living in sin?
If you'd ask their neighbors,
    most of whom belong to their parish,
    they'd tell you that these people
    are solid, good people.
They contribute to the public good,
    they care for each another
    and for others.
They have a great bunch of kids.
    They're honest, straightforward,
    loving, caring folks.

But they *are* public sinners
    because they have not formally
    reconciled with the church.

And last year when their oldest son
    received first communion
    in the church,
    they came forward with him,
    but they did not receive themselves.
They didn't receive
    because they couldn't receive
    because they aren't in union
        with the church.

There are many people like this today.
Some have simply made the decision
    to return on their own;
    some stay away;
    some have given up hope;
    most don't know what to do.

I wonder who the real public sinners are.
    Is a nuclear bomb builder a public sinner?
    How about the overly wealthy,
        the ones who hoard money?
    What about abortionists?

We can plainly see here
    that what is and what is not a sin
    is unclear today.
There are more questions about this
    than answers at the moment,
    and perhaps that's where we have to leave it.

Nonetheless, a couple of things *are* clear,
    abundantly clear.
First, sin is a reality
    and we are part of that.
Whatever its cause or its cure,
    sin is real
    and sometimes forcefully so.
We cannot set clear lines of definition
    about it,
    but that by no means
    makes it less real for us.

Second, the laws about sin
    are written on our hearts,
    and that's one of the centerpoints
    of the Good News.
We know.
Deep down, we know what is sinful
    and what isn't.

And when we realize that what we've done
    is sinful,
    we cannot avoid ourselves for long.
It haunts us;
    the healthy guilt we feel
    lets us know consciously
    what our hearts are telling us
        unconsciously
        about what we've done.
This law is not written on stone,
    as Jeremiah reported,
    but on our hearts.

Third, and most important in all of this:
    the heart of the Lord
    is mercy.
Listen to those words again:
The heart of the Lord is mercy,
    and in that is our real hope.
In that is our only way to health.
    It is our balm.
    It is our salve,
        our salvation.

We are talking here,
    don't forget,
    about the sacrament of penance.
We're talking about people going to confession,
    something which most people
    have simply quit doing.
What will our answer be?
Should we urge people to go back
    to the frequent practice of confession?
Or should we just accept the status quo
    and let people do what they do?

I have to tell you,
    I think confession is an important part
    of the spiritual life.

It cleans out our closets
and airs out the soul.
It keeps secrets from festering,
secrets that can kill.
It provides a chance to start over
after the many and continuous failures
that everyone experiences
in trying to be our best.
It opens the windows of the heart
and gives grace a chance to transform
reform
and conform us to our real selves.
I like it.

But I think
that there isn't one way to do this
which is better than any other.
For different sins,
different levels of sinfulness,
there need to be different ways
for us to confess
and move on to wholeness and grace.

So, for example,
for the kind of social sin
we talked about above,
it would probably be best
not to use the reconciliation room.
When we become aware of our
brothers and sisters in need
and our ability to help them,
as I did in front of my TV that night,
then the time for prayer is over,
and we should get to work
and get something done.
That is the form of reconciliation
that we should use
in that situation.
This is the form that

most closely meets the demand
of the Scriptures.

Or if we finally see that violence
is not of God,
but that we are
and we are committed to doing something
to show our belief,
we should find ourselves
on a picket line
or at a caucus
or somewhere that counts.
Hanging around a reconciliation room
confessing to complicity in nuclear war
will not end nuclear war.
Real reconciliation will cause us
to amend our lives
as well as our society.

Then for sins within the family,
or among our friends,
like lying
or fighting
or angry outbursts
or hurtful words
it might help to tell the priest about it,
but what is really needed
is family peacemaking.
For many sins like that
we needn't go to a priest,
but rather to the one we hurt
to ask for forgiveness.
That would be real reconciliation
because it would cause us
to amend our lives.

For the general sinfulness of our lives,
the day-to-day selfishness
and omission

and lack of prayer time
and so forth,
we have the rite of the Mass.
What could be more a reconciliation
than that?
The prayer of consecration
is explicit:
"This is the blood of the new
and everlasting covenant.
It shall be shed for you and for many
so that sins may be forgiven."
How much more reconciliation
do we really need than that?

Sometimes we need to sit down
with our pastor,
with the one who is our guide
in the spiritual life,
and lay it all out.
I think of this time
as a "fifth step"
for the life of faith
where we become willing to acknowledge
before God and another human being
the exact nature of our wrongs.
We need to do this;
without it we will begin to fudge.
We need to be honest and open
about our inner condition
that leads us to choose
death rather than life,
despair rather than hope,
the lie rather than the truth.
We need to say it out loud
because that makes it real for us
rather than hidden.

There are other ways for us
to seek reconciliation as well:

almsgiving
prayer
leading another sinner to Christ
fasting and abstinence
forgiving others.

And for the so-called public sinners,
    those who live outside our norms
    and who want to return,
    can we find a way for them to come home?
Can we find a method for reconciliation
    that is at least as merciful as Christ?

These are all adaptations
    of the sacrament;
    these are ancient and modern
    ways for us to seek reconciliation.
The point here is that we do need
    to process our lives
    and be aware of our sinfulness.
We do need to pray for forgiveness,
    to forgive others,
    and to praise God
        for the unconditionality
        the constancy
        the fullness of love
            that is ours in Christ.
We need a fearless and searching honesty
    about ourselves
    and we need to take that to another person
    to talk about it.
That other person
    will usually be a spouse
        a friend
        a trusted confidant
        or a spiritual director.
It will not necessarily be a priest.

But this doesn't diminish our need

for a sacramental celebration
of reconciliation.
We still need to gather
and acknowledge to one another
our need for forgiveness.
We will need the grace that is ours
only in this sacramental moment.
We need the absolute assurance
of hope and love,
of unconditionality,
of a continuous flow of grace.
We need, in a word,
the absolution of this sacrament.
We are human, after all,
and have a need for
visible,
tangible,
audible signs of God's love.

What does the future hold for this
holy moment in people's lives?

Many people have stopped using
this sacrament today.
But I simply do not believe
that these people are immune
to their sinfulness.
The rite of individual confession
to a priest
is not working for very many,
and we must be more honest about that.
It's an ideal rite,
one that we wish could work better.
But the experience of the people
was this:
As soon as it dawned on folks
that individual confession to a priest
seemed optional, they quit going.
They quit in huge numbers
and they quit immediately.

Does that tell us anything about the rite?
In seeing this happen,
      the tendency is to blame the people
      for having a shallow appreciation of sin.
"They aren't going to confession anymore
      because they don't believe in sin."
I think that's simply too easy an answer
      to a much more complex difficulty
      that people face today
      in dealing with sin,
            personal
            social
            and public
                  in their lives.
We must be much more concerned
      that the people of the community of God
      find ways to deal with their sinfulness
            which work
      than that they line up outside
            a room at church
            on Saturday afternoon.
We must be more concerned
      with people returning
      to Christ
      with all their heart
      rather than with numbers of persons
            fulfilling a prescription of the law
            about annual confession.
We could, for example,
      assist in this sacramental need
      by teaching folks
      to act as reconcilers and healers
            for one another
      to be good listeners
      to challenge one another
            and to challenge society at large
            to a fuller life of faith.
And we could continue to offer them
      gatherings for reconciliation

that use a form other than
individual confession to a priest.
We need the grace
of that sacramental moment.
We need to be urged and challenged
to be reconcilers
among each other
in our society
within our own selves.

If there is a sacrament
we badly need today,
it is this one.
We live in a time when sin
threatens to overtake the world
and destroy it
in thermonuclear war
in the starvation of thousands
in the acceptance of lying
in public in rampant sexual exploitation
in children rejected in the womb
in uncontrolled consumerism
in the pursuit of greed as a god
and in countless wars around the world.

If the formal rite of individual confession
is not sufficient for our time,
we cannot allow this
to prevent us from praying for forgiveness
and knowing God's love
and sharing that with others.
The time may have come when we must
decentralize this holy moment,
declericalize it,
and legitimatize people praying with each other
for forgiveness.
We need to get back
to being a people of faith,
the followers of Jesus,

who experience reconciliation
in our everyday lives.
What will the future of this sacrament be?
We should place this question
on every parish council agenda.
We should ask it of ourselves honestly
and earnestly
because this is one sacrament
that has the power to deeply transform us.
That transformation is the seed
of the peace of the world.
"The reign of God is within...and among you."

For Reflection and Discussion

1. What has been your honest recent experience of this sacrament? (pp. 96–102)
2. What role does adherence to the law play in determining what is personally sinful? (pp. 103–108)
3. What responsibility do we have for the greater social sins of our time? (pp. 108–111)
4. Who are the "public sinners" of your parish or family? (pp. 111–113)
5. How can the use of this sacrament be improved and strengthened in this parish? (pp. 115–122) What parts of the rite could be adapted to better fit our times?

Marriage

Among the sacraments,
    none has fared more poorly
    than matrimony.
The troubles with this sacrament
    began in the Garden of Eden
    and haven't really let up since.
More accurately,
    its troubles began
    with the telling of that story,
    in which it *appears*
    that the woman was created
        as a servant to the man,
        a sort of afterthought,
        someone to bear the children.
Actually,
    the storyteller there
    gave us a perfect model
    of relationship between married people
        when he said that
        they had become "one flesh."
Could there be any greater union?

They had the blessing of God
    to be fruitful and multiply,
    to be companions for each other,
    and to live in harmony with
        their environment forever.
Could there be any greater blessing?

But this storyteller
    was situated in an ancient world
    where women were the property of men.

So the story told
        reflects a cultural condition
                of dominance.
In fact,
        the only permitted sexual ownership
        was that one:
        man owns woman.
This ownership was more than sexual access:
        it was heirs,
        future ownership of land and flocks,
        and the assurance of children
                to carry on after one's own death.
The ancient world was much more frank
        about this than we are.

Ancient peoples lived in "households"
        which were headed by the owner
        and included slaves,
                relatives
                hangers-on
                and wives.
The owner was master of the house
        and master of the wives.
Nearly everyone was attached
        to some kind of household.
        That was how they lived.

The command not to commit adultery,
        as it was given to Moses,
        was given into this culture
        and sounds more like a command about
        these households
        than about sexual morality
                or loving relationships:
"You shall not covet your neighbor's wife."
It sounds as though
        she is about equal
        to thy neighbor's goods,
        which are mentioned first.

The text actually reads like this:
  "You shall not covet your neighbor's *house*;
  you shall not covet your neighbor's wife
  or his manservant
  or his maidservant
      or his ox or his ass
      or anything that is your neighbor's."
The wife in this command
  is listed after the property
  but before the slaves and beasts,
  which reflects the thought of that day.
Clearly she is treated as property.

For Job, then,
  the tragedy of adultery
  was not the loss of a loving relationship,
  but the loss of property.

We still see vestiges of this thinking today,
  of course,
  especially in our marriage customs.
The bride, for example,
  is often still given by her father
  to another man, her husband-to-be:
      one man giving a woman to another man
      sounds like an ownership exchange.
She is often veiled, presumed a virgin,
  while the male is not.
And most oddly of all (in our culture),
  the woman is expected to change her very name
  and take that of the man.
She gives away what is most personal
  and what is most "herself,"
      and becomes his
  while no one would ever expect a man
      to do the same for his wife.
A man who would do that would be
  thought to be odd.
The woman changes her name, we say,

because it's handy for naming the kids,
but I don't buy it.
A woman, especially in marriage,
does not become the property of a man,
ever. Period.
Where the name change doesn't imply that,
no problem;
but where it does, watch out!

But the ancient world
was not concerned with these things
as we are.
In that time,
which includes the time of Jesus,
most women were owned by their husbands.
Pitched against this backdrop,
then,
Jesus' command against divorce
flies in the face of contemporary custom
and does so vigorously.
Women, he was saying,
are not to be traded like oxen.
They cannot simply be taken and given,
willy-nilly,
in divorce.
Indeed, the hallmark of the gospel
was Jesus' preaching on love,
not only of men,
for God's sake,
but also of women.
Jesus himself showed this
by openly and lovingly embracing women
as his followers
in an age when that would have been seen
as ridiculous.
Those passages about his visits with women
come and go rather quickly
when we read the text
from our twentieth-century perspective.

But there is no doubt
    that they were radical in their day.
When Jesus invites us into relationship,
    he is inviting all of us
    without putting any one of us first.
That is,
    he treats women and men quite equally,
    no matter what the custom of his day.

So his teaching on divorce
    is a deepening of the concept of marriage,
    an insistence on the oneness
    between the partners.

But there does lurk an ambivalence
    about marriage in the Scriptures,
    especially in Paul.
This ambivalence seems to spring
    from his own view,
    apparently mistaken,
    that the end of the world was near
    and that we shouldn't waste time
        fooling around with marriage
        at a time like this.
Despite the fact
    that it was wedding feasts
    that were the stage of miracles,
        parables,
        and metaphors of the kingdom,
    Paul seems tough on it.
But he doesn't hold a candle to what followed
    in the church.
This poor attitude toward marriage
    reached a full development
    in Augustine.
For him,
    the purpose of marriage
    was soley the begetting of children
     which, unfortunately,
    requires sex.

Augustine didn't think much of sex,
      or rather he thought about it a lot,
      but he considered it evil.
He linked sex with animals
      and considered marriage tolerable
      as a means of keeping
      "perverse desire within its proper bounds."
This seems like a far cry
      from the God of Creation
      commanding us to be fruitful
            as a blessing,
      commanding us to enjoy creation
            because it is good.
It seems a far cry
      from the Creator
      who thought up the whole idea
            of sexual pleasure.
The loving God who crowned all of creation
      with human beings
      is the one who made being together
      such a pleasure.
This is the God who created us in the divine image,
      and who implanted within us a deep desire
            to be together,
            to gaze upon one another,
            to touch, hold, and love,
      and who provided us with partners
            for the purpose of doing just that.

This view, though,
      that there is something
            inherently inferior
            about marriage,
      dominated in church teaching
      for centuries
      and is still present today.
Further roots of our modern approach to this
      seem clearly to be in a contorted thinker
      of the seventeenth century
      whose name was Cornelius Jansen.

He believed, with others,
    that original sin has so corrupted
    human nature
    that it would follow without question
    that everything purely natural is evil,
        first and foremost, sex.
Grace, in his thinking,
    is difficult to obtain
    and given only to a few.
Because of this,
    Jansen believed and taught fervently
    that physical affection
        always borders on the sinful
        and usually *is* sinful.
He also believed that
    we should receive communion
    only very infrequently
    and only after a rigorous confession.

This thinking, called Jansenism,
    spread throughout France and Ireland
    and came from there to the United States
    with the great immigrations
        of the last century.

You can easily see
    that much of our
    obsession with sexual morality
    and our narrow eucharistic piety
        came directly from Jansenism.
This all added to an equally narrow view
    of marriage
    and an exalted view of celibacy.

The whole thing reached a sort of high point,
    or maybe a low point,
    in the tenth canon on marriage
    of the Council of Trent:
"If anyone says that...
    it is not better and happier

to remain in virginity and celibacy
than to be united in matrimony,
anathema sit!"
"*Anathema sit,*" in case the term
is not familiar to you,
means, literally,
"Let him or her be damned!"
Strong language, that,
to describe those
who favor marriage over celibacy.
Is it any wonder
that this sacrament
has fared so poorly
in catechesis and spirituality?
Is it any wonder
that the breakdown of marriage
has been so widespread?
Perhaps rather than bemoaning
the decline of lifetime marital commitment,
we should re-think
the church's approach
to this sacrament.
Maybe we ourselves have been part of the problem.

Vatican II has begun that re-thinking.
"The true practice of conjugal love,"
the Council documents say
in reference to marriage,
"and the whole tenor of family life
resulting from it,
tend to dispose the spouses
to cooperate generously
with the love of the Creator and Savior."
Doesn't that have an entirely different sound
than "*anathema sit*"?

Here sexual loving and the mutual love
of the couple
is seen as integral to family life
and human happiness.

Here there is respect and admiration
for the created and natural
role of sex in life.
Here there is returned to our thinking
a nobility to marriage,
a holiness,
an expression of God's love.
In the Council writings,
we see that marriage and celibacy
must function with each other,
neither more noble nor less
than the other.

The work at Vatican II
went a long way toward restoring
God's purpose for marriage.
We can plainly see here
the groundwork
for a spirituality of marriage
which makes it a central sacrament
in the whole church.
Just as the establishment
of human relationships
was the pinnacle of the creation story
in Genesis,
so living in and expressing that bonding
is the pinnacle of life in the church.
Two persons
who love one another deeply
know that the energy of their love
comes from God
and ultimately returns to God.
When they lie naked together in love,
expressing the highest human emotion,
taking the ultimate human risk,
and sharing the greatest human pleasure,
they enter into divine energy.
In a word,
when two loving persons have sex together,

then that is the most sacramental moment
    of human existence in the world.

There has also been widespread
    examination of Scripture
    in the last seventy or more years
    that has helped us to shift ground
    in our understanding of original sin.
This is important
    because our understanding
    of original sin
    is very much at the heart
        of our official disgust
        for things sexual.

Jansen was wrong.
We no longer believe, as he did,
    that the story of the
    sin of the first woman and man
        is factual history.
It is a Hebrew story
    intended to help us understand
    at least a little,
    how misery and evil have come into
        human experience.
It's a story intended to giving meaning,
    not facts,
    about human existence in the world.
It is creation mythology,
    not that different from
    and functioning for us
    just like the creation stories
    of native peoples everywhere.

Almost surely, we would say,
    the notion that human nature is evil
    no longer springs from this story.
Much to the contrary,
    we have in Scripture
    the human incarnation of Jesus Christ.

Human nature, if anything,
    is glorious in Christ!
"He did not deem equality with God,"
    the text says,
      "a thing to be grasped."
"Rather, he emptied himself,
    taking the form of a servant,
      being born in the likeness of humans."
Being fully human
    was Jesus' path to holiness.

It is also ours.

Today we look to sociologists
    and psychologists
    to help us understand the patterns
      and problems
      in human bonding.
We are learning to trust their work
    and to hear what they say
    as part of the unfolding
    of the truth
      in the human family.
Their contribution to this search for truth
    is invaluable for us
    in understanding human evil
      as well as human good.
We know from this
    and from our own common sense
    that for two people in love
    having sex is not purely biological.
There is a spiritual aspect
    that is present in this level of sharing
    which elevates the couple
      and energizes them.
This spiritual energy that is shared
    in marriage
    is that energy of love
    of which Jesus spoke:
"I call you friends," he said,

"because I have revealed myself
entirely to you."
"So this is my desire for you,
my command:
love one another likewise."
"As I have done,
so you must also do."

What happened in the Garden
with the "first couple"
was a rupture in their relationship.
They had been naked together,
without shame,
hiding nothing from one another.
They had lived, as the story goes,
in perfect relationship together.
But then they acted,
not relationally,
but unilaterally.
They acted selfishly.
And the rupture that resulted
divided them,
made them feel shame,
caused them to hide themselves
from each other
and from God.
That ruptured relationship,
symbolized in the taking of the fruit,
is the "first sin."

But marriage,
where two people share themselves
so completely
that they are emotionally
and spiritually naked together;
marriage where two people act,
not unilaterally,
but relationally;
marriage where the ultimate expression

of this caring and relationship
is found in their sexual union;
marriage restores the created order
and its highest act,
sex,
is the ultimate sacrament of God.

It is the consummation of creation,
salvation,
liturgy,
and gospel love.
And when this being-together-in-sex
results in the new life of a child,
the great creative power of God
is expressed as powerfully
as it was on the first day of creation.
The circle is complete then.
From the energy of love
emerges an object of love: the child.
The child is conceived in this loving moment
and will itself be loving because of that.

So when two people come to the altar
and to the community
asking to be recognized as married,
there is a great deal more going on
than a legal contract.
It is a great act of worship,
a profound expression of faith,
a tremendous sign of unity.
The wedding doesn't create the marriage.
The wedding celebrates a condition of unity
between the couple
that is already there.

Two people meet and begin to relate.
Somewhere down the line
in their being together,
they realize that they *are* married.

Marriage happens slowly,
    over many months and years
    through thick and thin
    in sickness and in health
    in good times and in bad.
Marriage emerges between people
    who share their lives,
        the ins and outs,
        the ups and downs,
    until finally they realize one day
    that it has happened:
    They have become married.
That is the point in their friendship
    when it's time to plan the wedding.
A wedding celebrates in several hours
    what a lifetime will produce.
This wedding, then,
    is a sign of a great deal more,
    and principally, it is a sign
        of the energy of divine love
        present again in the world!
What a moment of hope for us!

So, once a marriage has emerged,
    once the bonding has been deepened,
    once the sacrament is present—
        the sign of divine love—
        it really cannot be broken.
Whatever happened in the Garden
    to cause that rupture
    has been undone now
    and the mission of Christ
        is complete.
When we gather to witness a marriage,
    we are bringing together people
    whose common hope is in the couple.
These people are the church, after all,
    and they are expressing a unity
    for which we dream.
It is a tremendous mystery,

whatever it is that makes this possible
between us,
a great and holy mystery.
But it is a mystery we share together.
We gather for weddings because we have to.
Alone we have no strength;
we need one another to give clearer meaning,
greater wholeness,
a deeper experience of God.
In a word,
we must have each other
in order to have God.

But, of course,
sometimes marriages don't work out.
We are, after all, human as well as divine
in our loving.
Love is lovely, but sin is also real.

Sin can sometimes be a personal decision
to do what we know is wrong.
This is a conscious, willful choice
made by someone;
it results in personal sin.
But there is another,
more insidious kind of sin,
which is more common, really,
and more difficult to detect.
These are attitudes, motives, social conditions,
and old habits of thinking
which linger and which can also
vigorously contradict God's will.
They are our *unconscious* ways of acting,
the sleeping giant within us
that threatens to overpower us from within.
A pious religious person, for example,
as Mackin has pointed out,
may deny employee rights and pay slave wages.
A truly devout man

may continue to oppress women,
treating them as inferior to himself.
An entire country may continue
to import foods from Central America
at prices which leave those people
in perpetual poverty.
An economy may be managed by Christians
that, by its very workings,
creates destitute people within it.
Well-meaning people may continue to build weapons
known to hold the potential
for ultimate human destruction.
A culture may bask in its material wealth,
advertising a standard of living
that drives its own people to
a greedy way of living
that separates families and spouses.

No one in these cases seems to act consciously,
but nonetheless we are describing
a sinful situation here.

There seems to be just such an unconscious
lingering,
invisible force
at the heart of the breakdown of love.
We cannot reduce all marital breakdown
to one cause, of course,
but we can say with some certainty
that what we are pointing to here
is common.
We can say that it appears to underpin
much of what people pass through
as they find their love "gone cold."
We can say that this is true.

What is it? It's hard to describe.
We will call it,
with hesitancy, "flight from death."
I am hesitant to give it this name

because our fear of death is so great
that many readers will not go on
or, if they do read on,
     they will not listen to the text.
There is something a little grim about death.
We fear and hate it
     because it happens without warning
          so often.
It can happen just any old time,
     and it is so damn final for us.
It's also something that we know,
     deep down,
     we will have to pass through alone.
Not even the person we love the most
     will be there for us then.
When death comes to us,
     we will die alone.
Death is death; that's all there is to it.
But our real fear of death
     has more to do with the sense
     that when we die,
     we lose ourselves.
But that, you see,
     is precisely where the energy
     of the risen Lord takes hold for us.
Freely accepting death,
     daily dyings and lifetime endings,
     will free us for life.

Whenever we talk about this,
     someone in the crowd will always say,
     sounding as confident as possible,
     that he or she really doesn't fear death.
I hope that is true for them,
     and I know it is possible
     to embrace death as part of life
     and not live with this demanding fear
          in our hearts.
But many people who deny their fear of death
     are really filled with this fear.

What we fear about it
    is that we haven't lived enough to die.
We fear that we've blown this one chance
    for life.
We fear that we haven't been great enough,
    or happy enough,
    or that we haven't gotten enough gusto!
But when we go for that gusto,
    when we set out to really live,
    we often recoil in another kind of fear.
That other fear
    is the fear of looking foolish.
It's the fear of being criticized,
    of not being perfect,
    of not being right,
    of not being judged as normal.
In a word,
    it's the fear of living in the first place.
We fear death
    because we fear life.

These two fears,
    the one of dying
    and the one of living,
    prevent us from doing the one thing
        we most want to do.
They prevent us from giving ourselves in love.
What we most want,
    what we ache for in our guts,
    is to donate ourselves to others.
This donation of self
    is our created purpose,
    our saved purpose,
    what we're empowered for in life.
But because we fear that we will lose ourselves
    if we give ourselves away,
    we cling to ourselves desperately,
        selfishly,
        vigorously
    rather than giving ourselves away.

Even married people do this,
    frequently.
This is the basis of marital breakdown
    as well as the breakdown of friendships
    and family ties.
This is it: We fear what we want
    and we live in this fear
    rather than in love.

John talked of this in his letter:
    "There is no fear in love,
    perfect love casts out fear..."
But this, my friends,
    is precisely the grace of the sacrament
    of marriage in the church.
This is its point:
    we are empowered to love,
    not to hold ourselves away from real love.
We are made for this alone:
    to love one another
    as Christ loves us, the church.
When we gather in the power of Christ
    and we recognize that great death
    which has freed us to live,
    we are energized by his power.
We said earlier that what happens
    at a wedding is not simply a legal bond
    but a great deal more.
We can now see that what happens
    at this moment is an in-breaking of God
        an invitation to love,
            an intimate donation of God's own self.

So as two people proceed from their wedding day,
    they do so with this love.
They proceed with the power to embrace death,
    the daily dyings of their lives,
    which lead ultimately to the death
        of their bodies.

It is when they die for each other
    on a daily basis,
    even an hourly basis,
    that love will succeed,
    that death will indeed be conquered.

What do we mean by this notion
    that we must die for each other?
We mean precisely that:
    we die.
This is tremendously important
    in understanding the grace of marriage
    and we should spend a little time with it
    before moving on.
Daily dying for each other has two forms:
    one is to receive
    and the other is to give.
We receive and we give four things:
    time
    self
    prayer
    money.
It's a real dying for us to receive
    someone else's self:
    to listen carefully as they speak,
    to receive them as they are,
    to quiet our own shouting heart
        long enough to really *hear*
        what they say.
In order to do this we must have time,
    lots of time to give.
We must have time for visiting,
    sharing,
    pillow talk, boat talk, or whatever.
But we also need courage
    because this kind of sharing
    is so frightening for us.
We fear it because the other person
    sort of becomes naked before us.

He or she takes off the masks
    and tells the whole truth.
We have a lingering kind of discomfort
    with this.
    People often feel that there are some things
    that you just should never share.
They feel that becoming completely honest
    will somehow harm a friendship
    or challenge a marriage.
This is a radical form of death:
    we give ourselves to someone else
    and allow that someone else
    to be the guardian of our Self.
It is a great risk
    and has a lifelong effect
    any time it's done.

This is, in a sense, receiving the prayer
    of our beloved,
    for it is receiving their deepest self.
And it naturally follows
    that whatever other resources we have,
    money, property, whatever,
    would also be donated to the beloved.
Everything else, every other concern,
    takes a second place to this one:
    that we give and receive each other.

This emotional and spiritual nakedness,
    as we said earlier,
    is what sets the stage for
    and precedes the physical nakedness
        of sex.
We often call having sex "making love,"
    but we should really call it
    "celebrating love"
    because that's more accurately the truth.
Anybody can take off their clothes,
    but taking off our masks is another thing
    and is a dying second to none in life.

So the daily dying of love
    is the giving and taking of ourselves:
        our time
        our money
        our prayer
        our very Self.
We fear this kind of dying,
    for we fear that we cannot give and receive
    with grace.
We fear it, but we know
    that this is the risk we must take
    if love is to prosper for us.
And we enter into this because
    it's the way to truly live.

In this sense, then,
    our death determines our way of living.
We live in lieu of our death,
    and that shapes our life.
This makes it possible for us to know
    that we are living as we are created to live,
    that we are enough for now,
    that we do not lose ourselves in death,
        we gain ourselves.
That is the lesson of Christ:
    We really haven't lived,
        not completely,
        until we've died.
Death is part of life,
    part of daily life,
    and the grace of marriage
    is the grace to allow ourselves
        to die.

What does the future hold
    for this holy moment of life?
How will bonding be celebrated?
    How will the grace be recognized?

What is there in this sacrament
   and the power of this love
   that we should restrict the ordained
      from living in marriage?
And what is there here that we should prevent
   homosexual men and women
      from entering into lifetime commitments
      such as these?
What do we fear in this?
It seems to me that we should encourage,
   not discourage,
   lifetime commitments of love
   from the ordained and from homosexuals.
And finally, what is there here
   that we should not make every effort
   to help heterosexual couples
      deepen, strengthen, maintain
   and celebrate their own loving friendships?
The church, it seems to me,
   is these loving friendships.
And a crucial part of church liturgy is
   the working out of their lives
   the coming together of their hearts
   the daily dyings
   the emotional nakedness
   the spiritual power of love
   and the consummation of that love in sex.

For Reflection and Discussion

1. Is the body and its expression in sex morally good or morally evil? (pp. 123–133) Is celibacy or virginity a holier calling than marriage?

2. What is the difference between a marriage and a wedding? (pp. 133–137)

3. What does it mean to die to ourselves in marriage? (pp. 137–144)

4. What can this parish do to strengthen this sacrament? What parts of the rite could be adapted to better fit our times?

Holy Orders

It goes without saying today
    that the priesthood
    is in deep trouble.
Everyone can see that this is true,
    but almost no one will talk about it.
We need to be more frank
    for the sake of the church
    and for the sake of our priests.

An ordained friend of mine
    recently shared a story
    that helps us see the trouble clearly.
It seemed like "Catholic priest week"
    in the local papers,
    he told me,
    because there were several articles
        about priests asking to get out,
        about the general shortage
            of willing candidates,
        and about a local married ex-priest
            now doing pastoral work again.
But the most disturbing article
    had to do with sex.
It was also, of course,
    the talk of the town and the press.
Sex, a topic that isn't supposed
    to appear in the same paragraph
    with a priest's name,
        sex with an altar boy.
My friend read this along with everyone else,
    and he began to feel sad and alone;
        he felt as though everyone were

pointing to him, personally,
even though he was innocent.

With all these feelings in his heart,
he went off to his cabin
to cut some firewood.
While out alone and feeling better the next morning,
his neighbor came by,
someone he knew only in the context
of the cabin.
Without wasting too much time,
the topic of sex with altar boys was raised.
"You know," his neighbor said,
"It all kinda makes you wonder
about them priests."
Then, pausing, the neighbor realized
he was talking to one
and he added,
"Don't you wonder sometimes?"

Don't we all wonder sometimes?
The pastors of the church,
the ones charged with leading us to the Holy,
the all-important spiritual guides
in our communities,
the central figures in our parish life,
the men chosen for leadership,
are wondering, too.
Once the center of parish life,
today they are sometimes thought
to be standing in the way of progress there.
Once the most respected member of the community,
today they aren't trusted with our kids.
Once the ones we were sure would be there,
today we half expect them to leave.
Once the revered figure before whom we knelt
for a blessing,
today a confused person,
wondering about his own vocation
and his role in today's church.

In the changes made in the church
     after Vatican II,
     one of the major ones
     was the coming forth of lay people
          to work as ministers in the parish.
Many of the jobs that used to be done
     only by Father
     are now being done,
          willy-nilly,
          by any number of lay people:
Visiting the sick and imprisoned
     counselling the grieving
     preparation for marriage
     settling parish disputes
     deciding who can borrow the parish chairs
          where to put the flag in the sanctuary
          who should count the collection
          even who should sign the checks!
All of these are jobs now done commonly
     by ordinary lay people.

The one thing,
     the one and only thing,
     left exclusively to the ordained priest
     is to preside at the sacraments.
But even here change is creeping in.
The new code of church law,
     known as Canon Law,
     now permits that non-ordained people,
     that is, ordinary lay people,
          can, in some cases,
          baptize, marry, and bury.
So,
when it comes right down to it,
     what's left for the ordained priests
     is to preside at Mass and hear confessions.
Even the sacrament of anointing
     seems somehow less essential
     than it used to be.

This view—
    that all the ordained should do
    is to preside at Mass
        and hear confessions—
    is too narrow a view
    to be helpful to us today
in renewing the sacramental life of the church.
They have a far greater role
    which we will unfold here.
But first,
    let's take a look at what's happened
    in just the last twenty-five years
        regarding the role
        of the priest in parish life.

There was a time,
    within most of our memories,
    when a Catholic depended entirely
        on the word of the priest
        before anything religious
        was undertaken.
We didn't dare to use even a holy card
    without a blessing first
    from Father.
Priests,
    we believed,
    had some sort of immense, almost magical,
    spiritual power
        to bless or withhold blessing.
We believed that when they were ordained,
    they were somehow given
    a more direct line to God.

For North American Catholics
    this was especially true.
Except for the native peoples here,
    we were an immigrant people
    and we had little language, little money,
    little family,

little social power
     in America,
     a mainly Protestant nation.
America was founded,
     don't forget,
     by Protestants.
In fact, one of the goals of the early settlers
     was to escape the church of Europe
     which was struggling at that time
     in the aftermath of the Reformation.
The Puritans and Congregationalists,
     among the first Christians to settle here,
     sounded a Protestant anthem
     as they forged the early communities.
This land, they believed, was provided for them
     by God.
This was their land
     and, as they claimed it,
     America became predominantly Protestant.

But these immigrant Catholics
     were coming from places,
          Italy
          Poland
          Ireland
          France
          Spain
          eastern Europe,
that were mainly Catholic places.

They came here as immigrants
     to a place that was foreign to them
     and to a nation
     that wasn't sure it wanted them.
In fact, before long there were
     organized movements against the "papists."
As late as 1960,
     when John Kennedy was running
     for President,

Americans were wondering out loud
whether it would really be possible
to have a Catholic president
        without having the pope
        in control of the country.
(People who think this could happen
        don't know very much
        about North American Catholics:
                At this point,
                the pope would be happy
                to be in control of *the church* here
                much less the country.)

Their crossing of the Atlantic
        was as painful
        as their impoverished peasant lives
                in Europe had been.
They came with little family,
        from peasant villages
        where family life was central.
They came with little money,
        no land,
        no possessions,
        not even an ability to read.
They came with fearful hearts,
        escaping endless poverty at home,
        but they came alone.

These immigrants bore in their living
        a pain unimaginable today
        except when we look into the face
        of other displaced peoples.
Had they crossed the Atlantic today,
        riding in overcrowded quarters
        on lumber ship backhauls,
        we would have called them refugees.
Today we have Asians and Hispanics
        who are making this same voyage.
We often treat them

much as we ourselves were treated
when we were the immigrants.
We deny them rights
we assume for ourselves
question their willingness to work
avoid them
single them out
thankful that we aren't like them.
But they could be our parents or grandparents;
we *are* like them;
and we should never forget that.

So as they settled here,
the immigrants had to adjust:
to be Italian was to be Catholic
to be Irish was to be Catholic
to be Polish was to be Catholic.
But at that moment in history,
to be American was to be Protestant.

How did they cope?
To whom did these huddled masses turn?

They turned to the church
with a devotion and a zeal
unheard of since apostolic times.
The parish became the center of their lives,
and the priest was the center
of the parish.
Nearly every small town
and every city neighborhood
was ethnic in foundation.
And where that ethnic origin was
of Catholic stock,
they built a church first.
Protestant immigrants,
especially Scandinavians,
took the same course
as their Catholic neighbors,

often sharing the same small town
or city neighborhood.
The church became their protector,
their literal mighty fortress,
their gathering place,
a sociological center of life.

So this coming-to-America-as-immigrants
thrust us upon the church
for support.
And this is our point here:
It was the parish around which we organized
our whole lives
and the priest around which
we organized the whole parish.
We were the poorest class of people
in the country,
and we had the lowest level of education.
We came largely from peasant stock,
and we depended on our priests,
well educated
skilled in English
able to deal with the culture
leaders among the masses.

In this environment,
the priesthood flourished.
The seminaries were full,
ordination classes numbered in the dozens,
every family wanted a priest,
and every parish could have all it needed.
We built hundreds of seminaries,
and we sent our sons to fill them
in the thousands.
We built them and filled them
because to be a priest
was both a spiritual
and a social high point.
We built them in diocese after diocese

across the country,
and even when it began to be clear
that we could no longer fill them,
still we continued to build
in hopes that this "vocations crisis"
    would pass.
But it has not passed
    and our seminaries are empty.
Now they are chanceries,
    óffice buildings
    retreat centers
    nursing homes
    or empty shells.

Some had only one or two classes that graduated
    because the times changed
    before we did.
The priesthood began to disintegrate,
    and we allowed that to happen
    by our own false security about it.
We must have thought
    that it really wasn't happening.
We must have thought that
    the crisis would end shortly.
We could have seen it coming,
    but we were afraid to look.

The disintegration of the priesthood
    may have begun
    at Vatican II.
Xavier Rynne tells a story
    about the discussion at the Council
    of the document
    on the priesthood.
It happened in the fourth session,
    near the end of the entire Council.
The progressives
    who hoped for the reform
    of the priesthood
    were intending to provide

an exhaustive review of this office
as they had of bishop and lay person.
A debate was scheduled to occur
in the Council session
in accord with the routine working
of the Council's agenda.
The bishops and their theologians
were preparing for this discussion,
as they had for others,
by circulating position papers and proposals
informally in Rome.
At least some of these
called for a discussion about celibacy.

The conservative curialists were alarmed!

The evening before the debate was to occur,
one of the less progressive cardinals
dined privately with Pope Paul.
During dinner
he convinced the pope
to stall the discussion on celibacy
that surely would have been part of
that debate the following day.
The pope did so,
sending a letter to be read
the following morning before the debate began.
In this letter
the pope announced that he was
reserving to himself the right to decide
on the matter of celibacy
and that the discussion should not be held.
This took the wind out of the sails
of any who hoped for reform in
the priesthood.
The pope promised to deal with the matter
at a later time,
but no real reform has ever
come forward from anyone since.

The result has been devastating:
> We have bishops renewed in their
>> spirit
>> scope
>> approach
>> style
>> and support.
> We have a laity charged for ministry
>> ready
>> able
>> eager
>> and impatient.
> But we have a priesthood
>> unrenewed
>> dressed in black
>> alone in their rectories
>> paid a pittance
>> unsupported by anyone
>> generalists in an age of specialization
>> blamed for our failure to ordain women
>> on "call" twenty-four hours a day
>> addressed only by their title
>> expected to focus and foster
>>> the leadership of the laity
>>> which itself threatens
>>> their own very identity.

We have, in short,
> a renewed episcopacy,
> a renewed laity,
> and a medieval priesthood.

Now let me add an important footnote.
Many of the priests serving in the church today
> are healthy, well adjusted men
> who bring immense goodness and healing
> in their ministry.
Many are not threatened by the leadership
> of the laity.
Many are renewed indeed.

We are speaking here not of individual priests
    as much as of the priesthood
    as an office in the church.

In the past, as Jim Moudry has pointed out,
    the priest was seen as the
    unique and
    exclusive dispenser of
        sacred
        valued
        and needed functions in the community.
He was thought to possess certain sacred powers,
    as we have said,
    by virtue of his ordination.
This is changing today
    as we know,
    but we should be careful
        not to blame anyone
        for this dated understanding
            of priesthood.

Let's take a moment to
    survey some of the history
    of the "sacred powers" approach
    to the priesthood.
It grew slowly
    out of the feudel system in Europe
    seven hundred or more years ago.
Both Jim Moudry and Edward Schillebeeckx
    have done some very thorough work
    in studying this adaptation
    of the priesthood
    of the early church.

It's a complex story
    that we don't want to oversimplify,
    but our comments here will generalize
    and summarize nonetheless.

The roots of this have to do,
   in part, with money:
   the financial support of the clergy.
In the years of the early church,
   following the life of Jesus,
   leaders emerged from the community
      in which they worked.
It was pretty much the case then
   that priests were chosen as needed
   and supported financially by the community
   that chose them.
This traditional link to the community
   continued for a thousand or more years
   into medieval Europe
   but it took on the air of power
      as it aged.
The priest began to rule the community
   and its finances
   that formed his own personal support.
Then, as now, money talks
   and the one who governed the money
   governed everything.
So no one could be ordained who did not have
   a community willing to support him.
The priest was still closely linked
   to the community
   (he had to be or he didn't eat)
   but the linkage was less spiritual
   and more temporal.

This connection
   of the priest with the community
   followed a carefully laid out understanding
      from the earlier years
      of church history
      that ordained ministry
      was tightly linked
      to being called by a particular
         church community.

There was no such thing in those days
    as "absolute ordination."
That is,
    a priest wasn't ordained in general
    but was ordained for a particular place.
The community which he served continued
    to form part of his calling.
A priest did not have power
    except that he served
    a particular church community.
It was the people whom he served
    that empowered him for his work.
The call came from the community
    but was broadened to be representative
    of the whole church
    by the laying on of hands
    by the local bishops and priests.

But gradually this began to blur
    and soon we had priests ordained
    without a community.
They were ordained sort of at random,
    their ordination,
    rather than their link to a community,
    serving as the source of their power.
Their "power" of priesthood
    came then,
    not from the people
    but from other priests and bishops.
Added to the question of money
    and the support of the clergy
    was a renewal in the use of Roman law
    that allowed the development
    of the belief
    that there could be a fullness of power
        apart from the community.
This came, in time,
    to be seen as the power
    to consecrate the bread and wine
    at eucharistic gatherings.

It was a legal distinction,
    and it had nothing to do with theology.

Naturally, then,
    the power of the priesthood grew
    while the power of the laity diminished.

This would be enough of a problem,
    but it got worse
    as we began to enter a time when
    we began to believe
    that the world was in two realms:
        the spiritual
            where priests lived,
        and the secular,
            where the rest of us
            hung out.
So priests were holy and close to God,
    and the rest of us
    were not.

Once separated from the community like this,
    and set apart as holier
    than others,
        we can easily see
        how priesthood would begin to become
        a personal state of life
            a social status
            rather than a community service.

One of the central ingredients
    that made this work
    was celibacy,
    which was first made a law of the church
    in canons 6 and 7
    of the Second Lateran Council
    in 1139,
        (relatively recently
        from a Roman point of view).

It was made a law for priests in 1139,
    but there had been a practice
    of priests abstaining from sex
    the night before eucharist
    since the fourth century.
By itself,
    abstinence from sex before eucharist
    doesn't seem that it would be
    that much a burden
    for a married couple,
    except when you consider that
        at the same time,
        the practice of *daily* Mass
        began to be widespread.

What was the problem with sex and the eucharist?
First, from an ancient view of the matter,
    sex was seen as profane,
    not something that holy people
        would enter into,
        even married people.
It was carnal, earthy, messy, and unclean.

So, for the priest, as a sacred person,
    sexual abstinence was required.
The priest,
    after all,
    was the go-between,
        the intermediary,
        the only link
    between Christ and us.
He was a sort of
    "other Christ"
    in our communities.
And God knows,
    Jesus would never have had sex!
    Sex was thought to be sinful, after all.
There was an emerging belief
    that sex within marriage

should be tolerated at all
only as a way for people to
"relieve their concupiscence."
It was supposed to keep us
from becoming wild beasts,
sexually speaking.
Marriage could be tolerated for the weak,
but the really strong,
the really holy,
would have the inner strength
to refrain from sex,
something which obviously pleased God
more than enjoying sex did.
This was not strictly a Christian
point of view;
other local religions of antiquity
also had sexual laws
for their spiritual guides.
But for Christians,
anyone dealing directly with Christ
had better stay away
from all things unclean.

The other reason that celibacy worked so well
had more to do with money again.
Priests were, after all,
supported entirely by their communities,
and their support took the form of
what was called a benefice.
A benefice was a property with income
that often involved land,
a home,
maybe even slaves.
It simply wouldn't do
to have these benefices divided
among heirs to the local pastor.
It was much easier if he didn't have kids
hanging around to collect
the estate.

Now we must be clear in saying here
    that this inheritance factor
    had nothing to do with
    the rise of celibacy as a discipline
        for priests.
Nonetheless, celibacy was a
    convenient solution to that problem,
    and the church's resources increased
    dramatically after its imposition in 1139.

A footnote is in order about celibacy.
Among liberals today,
    celibacy usually takes quite a beating.
It's considered an unnecessary discipline,
    and one that should be made optional.
What we are saying here surely supports that,
    but celibacy can also be a wonderful gift
    in one's life.
For some, celibacy is not a burden but a calling,
    a vocation to a kind of freedom
        unstructured availability
        and absolute focus of attention
    that renders them more able
    to do God's work.
The argument is really not over celibacy as gift,
    but over whether every ordained person
    must have this gift.

Well, we've talked about sex
    and we've talked about money
    and we've talked about power.
Sex, money, and power—
    they often go together
    don't they?

Taken together, then,
    we had priests who could operate
        with no community to call them
    and a spiritual realm

into which common folks could not go
and a sacred power theology
that narrowed the view of priesthood.
You can plainly see
how we built our church hierarchy.
And,
as we said above,
in the immigrant North American church,
this was exaggerated
by the need of the community
for a social
as well as a spiritual leader:
our priest.

Now let me point out
that there is a natural human need
for spiritual leaders.
We have always had our
medicine men
sacred women
gurus
shamans
and guides
in the spiritual life.
Every culture and every religion has them.
If we did not have priests,
we would find others
to serve as our guides.
The guides we would choose would be
persons bound in our culture,
yet somehow able to transcend it.
They would be persons whose
insights
wisdom
leadership
and service
would naturally attract us.
They would be naturally spiritual people.

And they would not necessarily
　　be celibate men.

But in the pre-Vatican II period
　　of our American immigrant experience,
　　we could not have done that.
We needed our priests
　　and this form of priesthood
　　met our needs well.
Out of this came a heavy dominance
　　of the institutional model of the church.
That the church was also
　　the people of God,
　　the common people from the pews,
　　　　was unheard of.

But the times and the church have both changed.

Today the church is full of folks,
　　common lay folks,
　　giving their time and abilities
　　in leadership roles of all kinds.
Today parents have learned to
　　give blessings to their children.
Today everyone prays for
　　and celebrates forgiveness.
Today Father no longer keeps a
　　holy water vial nearby
　　in case someone needs a holy card blessed.
Instead,
　　he keeps the parish bulletin nearby
　　so that he can keep track of
　　all the prayer groups,
　　　　committees,
　　　　councils,
　　　　and coordinators
　　active and present in the parish.

The immigrant North American Catholics

placed their faith
in their priest and their church.
Today we have moved to a new place
and are concerned to place our
faith in the Lord,
who is beyond the priest
and beyond the church.

So the laity of the church
have come of age.
The essential sacrament of ministry today
is not seen to be ordination
but rather baptism.
Baptism empowers us for ministry.
Everyone has a ministry in the church,
we say today,
everyone has a role.

But, if this is true,
that everyone is called to ministry,
then what is left for the ordained ones?
What are they supposed to do
if someone else can proclaim
the readings at Mass?
if someone else can visit the sick?
if someone else can pray with the dying?
if someone else can prepare
young people for marriage?
if someone else can sign the checks?
Is there anything left
other than presiding at Mass,
doing what the liturgist tells you to do,
and hearing confessions
for those few who still go?
They might as well be lay people in the church—
at least that way
they could get married.

The answer to this begins in the

story of creation from the
Book of Genesis in the Bible.
There it says that,
"in the beginning
God created the heavens and the earth."
"The earth," the text says, "was without form."
It was,
in other words,
in chaos.
Everything was there that would be needed.
All the gifts were present,
but they were disorganized,
chaotic,
swirling about without order
and, therefore,
without meaning.
But then,
the text says,
"the Spirit of God
moved over the face of the waters..."
And in the very next breath of the text,
the very next verse,
the writer begins to unfold
the holy order
that God's Spirit brought about:
First the light,
then the wonderful order of the stars,
then the earth
with its incredible balance of resources.
Next there would be vegetation,
plants and animals,
all kinds of them,
in balance with each other
and the earth,
a wonderful divine ecology.
And finally,
the crowning moment,
the ultimate in the holy order of creation:
the human family,

each body carrying within
its cells
the code of life
present from the merging
of the first two cells
within the mother's womb.
All of this holy order
a gift from God
through the Spirit
that hovered over the chaos.

Well,
this helps give us a theology
of the priesthood
for today's church.
It is far more than
saying Mass and hearing confessions.
The priest is the one in the community
who brings holy order
into the many and varied gifts
of the members.
The priesthood is a gift of the Spirit
to a church
that would otherwise be in chaos
and sometimes is.
The priest, then,
as Jim Moudry has said so clearly,
is the "order bringer."
It is he who brings into concert and harmony
the gifts given by God
to each member,
including himself,
and who thereby
orchestrates the unfolding melodies
of the kingdom of God
present here,
present within us
shared among us.
In the very person of the priest,
God's spirit hovers among us.

The priest
    calls forth,
    fine tunes,
    and directs
        the work of the church.
He does not,
    thereby,
    perform all this work himself,
    but rather, he enables others to undertake
        their own work,
        all according to their gifts.
He is not the only such leader in a parish,
    but he is a distinct kind of leader there.
He is the leader among leaders,
    the pastoral leader.
Rather than being the possessor
    of sacred powers,
    he is the maker
        of sacred order.

This is the grace of the sacrament
    of holy orders
    in the church today.

Laying aside for the moment
    the question of who should
        or should not
        be ordained,
we can plainly see that we need this gift
    in the church
    and that we would be in chaos
        without it.
But we can also plainly see
    that we need more
    well-trained enablers today
    to take up and exercise this gift.
This is not priesthood for social status
    or for sacred power,
    this is priesthood for service.

This person, this priest,
    does also preside at public prayer
    in the church,
    but he does so now
        not because he holds some unique power
        to consecrate bread
        that no one else possesses,
    but because he is the one
    charged with ordering
        the life of the church.
A central aspect of bringing that order
    is to be a central figure,
        though again not the only figure,
        in public worship.

The words used to ordain a priest
    give us a deep insight into this reality.
The old words,
    before the renewal of Vatican II,
    read like this:,
        "Receive the power
        to proclaim the Gospel"
    and
        "Receive the power
        to offer the Mass."
A power was being passed
    from bishop to priest
    and this power seemed unrelated
        to the community.
But today the ordaining bishop says instead,
    "Receive the gospel of Christ
    and announce it faithfully."
        and
    "Receive the gifts from the people
    and do with them what you're supposed
        to do."
This new language does not suggest
    that a personal power
    is being given to the priest,

but rather,
    that he is called to a new level
    of leadership and service in the church.

Today we are no longer immigrants,
    and we do not treat the ordained priest
    with the he-can-do-no-wrong
    attitude we once did.
Today we see each other as ministers,
    sharing the work of God on earth.
But because of this,
    we have a great challenge:
How can we learn to support and affirm
    the ones who work among us
    as ordained priests?
How can we thank them adequately,
    challenge them gently,
    invite them generously into our communities?
What new relationship can we form
    for today's church
    that includes them
    without setting them apart?
At least some of those ordained ones
    in our midst are hurting,
    and we must find ways to heal that.

With these thoughts about holy orders
    behind us,
    what will the future hold for
        this sacrament?
What should our "personnel plan" look like
    for the future of our church?

I do not believe
    that the theology of this sacrament
    and the future of the community of Jesus
    suggest that we should wait
    for more celibate men to come forward.
We need a strong, healthy priesthood
    in the church today.

But who will these priests be?

There are those who claim that
    if only we restored the "old church,"
    we'd have all the priests we need.
There are those who claim that
    if only we'd ordained women
        and married persons,
    we'd have all the priests we need.
There are those who claim that
    maybe we don't need priests at all.

I don't take any of those positions.

The reforms of the priesthood
    which were not undertaken at Vatican II
    or anytime since
    are badly needed today and tomorrow.
Our tasks
    to witness to the truth
    to live a holy life
    to guide one another in faith
    to provide for one another's needs
    and to establish a reign of justice
        peace
        light
        goodness
        and beauty
requires leadership from somewhere.
We need an adequate number of leaders
    because already we see
    that everywhere in the church
    the people are being deprived of the eucharist
    which is the centerpost
        of our lives in Christ.
People are deprived because
    there aren't an adequate number of priests,
    and our response has been
    to wait for God to send more.

This stubborn waiting
    might almost be thought to be
    a blasphemy against the Holy Spirit
    who appears to be sending
        other workers into the harvest.

Our personnel plan seems not to fit
    very well with what is going on around us.
I think of Jesus describing the kingdom:
    You look into the western sky
    and see a cloudbank moving in,
    and you know that rain is coming,
        he said;
    how is it that you can read the signs
    in the skies so clearly,
    but you cannot see the signs of the kingdom
    which are all around you?!
I think we do not see who it is
    that God has sent.

The church today is filled with leaders,
    many of them well equipped,
        well educated in theology,
        well prepared for the task.
When such pastoral workers
    come forward
    to work in a parish
        a school
        a diocese,
        or wherever,
we accept them willingly,
    but we do not lay hands on them all.

Maybe we should.

Maybe being a priest isn't something
    that you can study to become;
    maybe it's something
    that you discover you are.

Maybe these pastoral workers
    some currently lay folks
    some ordained
are the ones God has sent to us.

Maybe our failure to notice their call,
    or, having noticed,
    to allow them to receive
    the ordination of the church,
maybe that failure is the real "crisis."

Maybe the reform of the priesthood
    is underway already
    guided by the Holy Spirit.

The community of Jesus
    has within it persons gifted for leadership.
These persons are not gifted
    by a local department store
    or a credit card company
    or a school of theology.
They are gifted by the Holy Spirit.
Why do we not turn to them?

For Reflection and Discussion

1. What is the role of the ordained priest in the church today? (pp. 164–169)
2. Who's in charge of this parish? (pp. 169–172)
3. How can we better support our priests today, given the difficult situations in which they must work?

Healing

Do you believe that God
    can heal your body when it's sick?
Do you think that God *wants* you
    to be sick sometimes?
Or does God want you to be well?

If you believe that God wants you to be sick,
    then why do you pray for healing?
Wouldn't it be against the will of God
    for you to be well
    if God wants you to be sick?

If God can heal you,
    then why doesn't God do that
    in all cases?
Why didn't Jesus heal the whole world,
    for that matter,
    while he had a chance
    when he lived in the first century?

Why do some people get well
    and others stay sick?
Why do even people who pray to get well
    often remain sick
    while others,
        people who are not even Christian,
        go on living healthy lives?

Are death and illness really punishment for sin?
Does God inflict illness upon us
    to punish us
    just as he made the Egyptians suffer

before they allowed the Israelites
to leave on their exodus?
But if illness is a punishment for sin,
then why do people who commit sins,
like murderers and rapists,
go on living healthy, normal lives
while God-fearing people get sick?
Would God be punishing a little child
who develops cancer?

Is God punishing a whole airplane load of people
who crash and die?
Is there some massive plan in the mind of God
that brought all those people together
in that one plane
to have them killed together
because he was finished with their lives?
If God is punishing us for sin or death
when we get sick,
then why doesn't God tell us
exactly what we're being punished for?
Or is it sort of "punishment in general"?

And what about healing?
How does all this work?

Are we begging God for wellness
like a child begs for candy
from an arbitrary parent
who won't give in?
Is there some special formula of words
we have to use
to convince God to make us well,
so that if we use just the right words
or do just the right sacrificial act
we will be made well?

Does God routinely intervene in human history

this way?
Does God arbitrarily make some people well
and others sick?
What's going on here?

One possible way to answer these tough questions
is to say, simply,
"This is all mystery;
it's all in the mind of God,
and who can understand that?"
"Everything that happens brings *some* good
to someone."
"God wants your dead child to be with him [sic]
in heaven."
"God is teaching you a lesson."
"God sent this tragedy into your life
because God loves you so much
and God wants you to be close to Jesus."
And finally,
"This is all in God's plan."

But these answers,
once given by pious teachers and pastors,
are no longer sufficient for us.

In a sense,
this is where our faith in God
really gets tested.
This is where the old sacramental rubber,
as they say,
really hits the road.
Can God heal us or not;
and if God can,
then why hasn't God done that?
Maybe God doesn't love us
or maybe, just maybe,
God can't really heal.

Before we talk specifically about

the sacrament of healing,
we should pause here just a moment
to think about our understanding of God.
Each of us has a notion
    of who God is,
    how God acts,
    why God does this but not that,
    and how God relates to us.
We have an idea about this
    which we have developed over the years
    as we have learned about God at church.
How we view God determines how we pray
    and what we believe about healing.

We take a lot of our understanding of God
    from the first century
    because that's when the gospels were written.
In that first-century time,
    people believed that the earth was flat.
The world was seen as three-storied,
    heaven was up
    hell was down
    and earth was in the middle.
God and the angels lived in heaven
    while hell was a place of torment
    where Satan and his agents lived.
Earth, the middle ground,
    was no ordinary place either.
Earth was seen as a battleground
    for God and Satan
    and all their agents.
It was believed that both of these
    supernatural beings, God and Satan,
    routinely intervened in human history.
They roamed the earth
    trying to win subjects to themselves.
Satan made people sick
    while God healed them.
Satan caused death and illness,

pain and suffering,
    sin and failure.
God was the source of Goodness
    Light
    Beauty
    and Truth.

A person could be possessed by these spirits,
    by God or by Satan.
Being possessed by evil spirits
    made a person sick or crippled
    and illness was seen in these terms.
Thus a sick person was thought
    to be possessed by evil spirits.
Jesus himself taught vigorously against
    this primitive belief,
    arguing that it isn't sin
    which makes a person ill.
But the popular belief of the day
    was that God and Satan
    acted in an arbitrary and capricious way,
    and one could never be quite sure
    which would overtake you next.

Into this world, then,
    this three-storied world
    with God and Satan doing battle
        for our souls,
    God sent Jesus.
Jesus "came down" from heaven to earth,
    taking the form of a human.
He was God present here,
    fighting against Satan
    by healing and teaching the truth.
He was killed as a criminal,
    buried,
    and later raised from the dead.
His previously dead corpse
    breathed again,

walked again,
and ate again.
God demanded this bloody sacrifice
of his own son
in order to forgive our sins.
Our sins were seen to be the reason
for the killing of Jesus.
After his death
Jesus descended into hell,
but this isn't all clear to us.
Sometime later Jesus rode triumphantly
on a cloud
up into heaven
where he is said to have a throne
of some kind.
His mother, Mary,
also went physically into this place
and is also there now.

This whole event of Jesus Christ
was seen as the beginning of the end
of the world.
Death was to be abolished,
Satan stripped of power.
We are waiting, according to this view,
for Christ to reappear,
riding upon the clouds,
to complete the work of redemption
in a final judgment
which will resemble a court of law.
Some will be found deserving,
but most will be damned.
Sin, suffering, and death will be abolished
once and for all
on this day,
and we expect this to happen quite soon.
St. Paul thought it would happen
before his own death,
and it seems certain that
Jesus shared that belief himself.

At the end time, as we expect it,
    the dead will come out of their graves
    and be taken, body and soul, into heaven
    and that will be that for the earth.

This is a first-century view
    of divine life and activity,
    but we have a more immediate question:
Who is God for us today
    and what do we really believe?
When we recite the creed at worship,
    what parts do we literally believe
    and what parts have we ourselves
        stopped believing as literally true?
An honest answer to these tough questions
    can leave us more deeply faithful
    than we ever imagined.
But the continued avoidance of them
    can leave us with faith
    in just so many empty words.

The sacrament of healing in the church,
    not well understood,
    mostly ignored,
    and largely avoided,
calls us to this deep level of belief.

It calls us to examine these realities
    of divine energy
    in our depths.

But in order to understand
    this important sacrament at all,
    we have to first respond
    to all those questions posed above.
We respond to them by saying
    that they are valid questions,
    but that they are asked in the wrong way.
They are asked as though an answer
    can be given

in the same way that we would answer
a problem in math,
  as though we can state
  in clear, certain words
  what God's activity is like.
We cannot.

Modern people want such answers,
  and they want them in modern language,
  but the questions themselves are posed
  in a first-century jargon
    which doesn't allow
    answers in twentieth-century language.
Asking how God acts from God's place in heaven
  is a first-century concern.
Asking about God's moods,
  ways to plead with God for healing,
  or continued life and safety
    are first-century concerns.
Asking about God's plan
  in terms of whether we live or die
  in illness or accidents
    is a first-century concern.
Asking about God's or Satan's movements
  from heaven or hell
  and their roaming about the earth
    is a first-century concern.

We have concerns today, too,
  and often we voice them in this language
  but when we do,
  we find that we don't have easy solutions
    because while we ask our questions
    in first-century language,
  we must answer them in our own.

We need not examine this view
  of the world, God and Satan,
  line by line, to know

that we do not hold
   that it is literally true.
It is a view of the world
   that comes from a pre-scientific age
   of human history.
The world is not flat;
   heaven is not, physically, upwards
   since there is no "up"
   that hasn't only hours before been "down"
   as the earth spins in space.
The stars are not demonic forces,
   and the earth is not a battleground
   for spirits competing for the souls of people.
The bodies of the dead have decomposed
   in their graves
   and will not come physically back to life.
The death of the body is not the result of sin;
   it is a part of how the earth is organized;
   it's a part of the cycle of life.
God does not live in a heaven
   physically located some place
   in reference to earth.
Satan does not rule a physical kingdom
   known as hell.
And do we really expect that Jesus
   ascends and descends on the clouds
   as though they were
      some sort of celestial elevator?
Finally,
   do we really believe
   that the physical corpse of Christ
   was raised again to life as we know it?
Did that physical corpse pass through walls,
   appear as a stranger walking to Emmaus,
   and eat fish in the upper room?
If so, where is it now?
Is resurrection about a physical return to life?

The more we discover about our universe,

our bodies,
and our earth,
 the less we attribute to God.

So what can we say about all this, then,
 in a way that will be meaningful
 for modern people,
  for us?
Let's begin by returning to a biblical story,
 the one about creation.
We should think about our own time
 as a part of that story.
The storyteller gives us a full view
 of the emergence of light
  darkness
  seas and land
  plant and animal life
  stars, planets, and moons
  fish, cattle, wild animals
  and, finally, humans.
I think it helps us to see
 that this whole process
 of creation and emergence
 is still going on.
It's a story, not intended to explain
 how it happened and was completed
 but rather how it *is happening*.
The earth continues to quake,
 continues to form new areas of sea
 and new configurations of land.
Animals and plants continue to grow
 and change;
 they continue to emerge in new forms.
And we humans are, too,
 in that sixth day of creation.
It isn't over for us;
 we continue to move toward wholeness,
 continue to learn more,
 continue to leap further each year.

God, as it were, isn't finished with us yet.

The whole movement of peoples
    and global development
    is in a discernable growth toward oneness.
Mass communications,
    rapid travel,
    global awareness:
        they all point to a coming-together
        by the human family.
We are learning that we are more
    like each other
        than different.
We are learning that we need to love one another
    more than we need to hate one another.
We are learning that we are not alone,
    perhaps not even in the universe.
And we are learning that
    we must share our resources,
    share our knowledge,
    share our growth
        so that we can all move forward
        as one.
We know that our failure to do this
    could produce great violence
    and possibly nuclear annihilation.

So it is with healing.

There is much that we are discovering.
The healing activity of God
        is found,
        in today's language,
    in the laboratory that searches for cures
    in the hospital that serves the sick
    in the psychologist
        who counsels toward wellness
    in the nursing staff that treats the patient
    in the spiritual guide
        who seeks meaning with the ill.

There is no dualism in our view.
God is present in the world
and the activities of humans
are filled with divine energy.

So, can God heal your body
when you're sick?
Yes, God is healing you through modern
medicine,
psychology,
and spirituality.
We are moving toward wholeness,
wellness,
and oneness.
And that movement,
when it is truly toward wholeness,
is also toward God
because God is One.

Does God use illness or death
to instruct us or punish us?
We would answer this by saying
that our biblical tradition
has continually centered on God
as Love.
This loving presence
is experienced as energy toward
relationship and unity,
again, toward oneness.
So if we develop lung cancer
because we smoked cigarettes,
we are being punished, I suspect,
but the punishment is our own,
not God's.
If we take up activities that threaten us,
then the results of that
will be illness and death.
And if we develop a disease
that seems to come from nowhere,

then we may find ourselves
part of the human family's
    yet unfinished growth,
    yet incomplete wholeness.

Like the other sacraments,
    prayer for healing
    has two effects:
It both helps us recognize the healing power
    present from God
    and also celebrates that healing.
The grace of this sacrament is peace:
    the peace of presence,
    the peace of death,
    the peace of knowing in our depths
        that creation is ordered by God,
        and we are moving with the river of life.
We are on our way
    and, even though not yet there,
        each moment of healing
        is another step.
We can take great heart in this,
    and we can know that God is with us.

More frequent teaching about this sacrament
    can help modern people
    grow in their faith.
It can endorse the healing arts and sciences;
    it can provide a faster movement
    toward health in our time.
It can uncover the barely known
    spiritual powers possessed by healers
        among us;
    it can help us trust those people
        able to heal.

This sacrament gives us an entry point
    to help modern people
    transfer their first-century notion of God

into a healthy twentieth-century
        experience of God.
It can help them to grow
    from a language of God "up there"
    to an experience of God in their depths.
It can provide a context for healing
    unprecedented in any previous age.

For Reflection and Discussion

1. Does God sometimes desire that you suffer illness, pain, or death? (pp. 175–177)

2. Where is God and how does God intervene in your life? (pp. 178–183)

3. How does the healing activity of God fit into our lives today? (pp. 184–188)

4. How can this parish better celebrate healing in this community? What parts of the rite could be adapted to better fit our times?

Five More Sacraments

Our lives are filled with holy moments.

We have talked about some of them
    here.
But we have also failed to mention
    some others,
    some which ought to be treated.
And there are some questions
    we must ask
    even about those we have discussed.

This will be a brief coda
    on the work we have just presented,
    but it takes its lead
    from the opening words
        of this project:
"No one is quite sure
    how many sacraments there really are."

There are other holy moments
    in human experience,
    and it seems fitting to think of them
    as sacraments, too.
Though they have never been included
    in the official lists,
    they seem very sacramental.

For example,
    the vowed life.
When a woman enters a religious community
    to become a sister

or a man, to become a brother
that moment is a holy one.
It is, really, a sacramental moment.

Here is a moment
that gathers up their whole life
and focuses it
on the community of God.
Here are people
willing to seek love in mystery,
living a single life of celibacy.
Here are people
offering unstructured availability
to us,
willing to meet whatever need arises.
Here are people
exchanging the goods of consumers
for the good of a simpler life.

How could this be more sacramental a moment?

Another moment like this,
one that more people experience frequently,
is the liturgy of the word.
Why is this not as sacramental
as that of the eucharist?
The "breaking of the word,"
the sharing of its depths,
and the sharing of our own responses,
is a very holy moment in life.
Just as the vowed life is a sign:
unconditonality in love,
availability in work,
and simplicity in living,
so the liturgy of the word is a sign:
the voice of the living God
calling us
forming us
and informing us constantly.

Here's another suggestion,
    maybe a tenth sacrament,
    after the vowed life and the word.
Why isn't almsgiving sacramental?

Almsgiving? you ask.
Do we want to dirty the sacraments
    by having one
    that deals with money?
Maybe we should.

We are learning something new
    about almsgiving in our day and
    in the first world cultures.
We are learning that it is a way
    for wealthy people (us)
    to organize our lives
    according to the gospel.
We are learning that
    we need to write our checks
    according to what we believe.
Money, it turns out,
    in our first world capitalist cultures
    has become a nasty replacement for God.
Greed is glorified;
    hoarding is acceptable;
    and success is measured in dollars.
But money itself is not the problem
    as much as our way of managing it is,
    and almsgiving provides
    a new management scheme for our money:
        give it away
        share it evenly
        there is plenty for all.
More people may come to Christ
    by giving away their money
    than through the other sacraments combined.
Let's think this over:
    maybe almsgiving should be a sacrament.

There is another possible candidate
        for placement as a sacrament:
        being part of and meeting with
            a base community.
Now this, I realize,
        is very close to my second suggestion,
        that of the liturgy of the word.
But this springs from the impact
        that the Latin American church
        has experienced from this new model
            or gathering style
            of the church there.
People who are part of these communities
        experience a profound power
        and presence,
        one that is very sacramental.
They make grace present in the world:
        the role of a sacrament.

All of these,
        and there are other good ideas, too,
        meet the test for sacraments:
            they have outward signs,
            they spring from Christ,
            and they provide grace.
They are already widespread practices
        in most of the church;
        and where they aren't,
        they should be.
If you take each of these
        and add one more idea,
        suggested by Edward Schillebeeckx,
        that Christ is the first sacrament,
        then we'd have twelve.
Having twelve would be a good idea
        because it would mean
        that we'd have to re-train
        the entire adult church
        that grew up thinking there were only seven.
I think this isn't a half-bad idea.

An Afterthought

One thing we can say for sure
    about the sacraments
    and this discussion:
    it will never end.
We will go on talking about these things
    for a long, long time.

That's probably a good thing;
    too much certainty
    should make us nervous.

So, really, there is no end here.
We need to keep going
    keep thinking
    keep talking
    keep arguing
    keep on truckin'!

Nonetheless,
    one last thought
    insists on being presented here:

The church is the people of God.
Therefore,
    the responsibility for reform and renewal
        of the sacraments,
        as George Worgul has said,
    must move beyond being the exclusive work
    of the clerical caste
    and its centralized committees.
This is our work,

all of us,
clerics and lay people together.
Each part of the body of Christ
plays an indispensible role
in invigorating these wonderful,
holy moments.
The drama of these sacraments
must reflect the drama of God's work
in our lives.
We must take this up,
every parish council,
every worship commission,
every family.
Declericalizing and decentralizing
the sacraments will not lead
to chaos.
We need not fear letting go
and allowing for the messiness
that will result from many hands.
Messiness will lead us, ultimately,
to a greater and more vigorous
sacramental life.
Nothing gets done,
don't forget,
until we get our hands dirty.

For Reflection and Discussion

Read:
"Five More Sacraments"
"An Afterthought"
1. What touched you most in these discussions?
2. What feeling or memory is more outstanding for you?
3. Which of the sacraments means more to you now?
4. About what in this do you feel hopeful?
5. How will you "get your hands dirty" in helping shape the future of the sacraments in your parish?